HARMONY OF THE CREATIVE WORD

HARMONY OF THE CREATIVE WORD

The Human Being and the Elemental, Animal, Plant and Mineral Kingdoms

Twelve lectures given in Dornach, Switzerland, between 19 October and 11 November 1923

RUDOLF STEINER

RUDOLF STEINER PRESS
LONDON

Translation revised by Matthew Barton

Rudolf Steiner Press
51 Queen Caroline Street
London W6 9QL

www.rudolfsteinerpress.com

Published by Rudolf Steiner Press 2001

First published in English as *Man as Symphony of the Creative Word* by
Rudolf Steiner Publishing Co., London (no date)
Second edition Rudolf Steiner Publishing Co. and Anthroposophic Press
1945
Third edition (translated by Judith Compton-Burnett) 1970, reprinted
1978
Fourth edition (revised by Anna Meuss and Karla Kiniger) 1991

Originally published in German under the title *Der Mensch als
Zusammenklang des schaffenden, bildenden und gestaltenden Weltenwortes*
(volume 230 in the *Rudolf Steiner Gesamtausgabe* or Collected Works) by
Rudolf Steiner Verlag, Dornach. This authorized translation is published
by kind permission of the Rudolf Steiner Nachlassverwaltung, Dornach

Translation © Rudolf Steiner Press 2001

A catalogue record for this book is available from the British Library

ISBN 1 85584 098 7

Cover illustration by Anne Stockton. Cover design by Andrew Morgan
Typeset by DP Photosetting, Aylesbury, Bucks.
Printed and bound in Great Britain by Cromwell Press Limited,
Trowbridge, Wilts.

Contents

Part Four
THE SECRETS OF THE HUMAN ORGANISM

Synopses

Lecture 1, 19 October 1923

Man as a microcosm. The bird is essentially head. Its plumage corresponds to the power of thinking in man. In the bird breathing dominates and lightens all other systems. In the lion there is balance between breathing and blood circulation. All parts of the lion reveal the mastery of the rhythmical system. The cow is all digestion, and a sublime astral principle has become flesh in it. Man is a harmonious synthesis of bird, lion and cow, in which creatures he also sees soul powers reflected. Gandhi and the cow. Stages in the development of the butterfly in relation to the sun. These stages compressed in the case of the bird. Bird plumage corresponds to momentary thoughts, the butterfly to memories. An African fable illuminates the poverty of logic.

Lecture 2, 20 October 1923

The sun in relation to the outer planets. It works on the eagle in connection with these, and especially Jupiter. The lion is pre-eminently the sun animal. The sun in connection with the inner planets works on the digestive processes, exemplified by the cow. Its forces also work through the earth and produce the heaviness in cow nature. The cosmic urge today to separate the three systems in man. The alluring calls of eagle, lion and cow, and their dangers for the West, Central Europe and the East. Possible mechanization of the earth and its consequences for the planetary system. A wrong way of using the secret of the cow. The counterparts to the animals in the African fable. The fable retold for modern times. The right answer of man to the three alluring calls.

Lecture 3, 21 October 1923

Physical and spiritual substance. Spiritual substance predominates in the lower organization of man (limbs), physical substance in the upper (head). Distinction between substance and forces. In the head, forces are spiritual, in the limb system, physical. Use of this knowledge in medicine. Man's twofold debt to the earth in that he takes into death spiritual substance (of limbs) which the earth needs, and leaves behind physical substance (of head) that he has estranged from the earth. This causes pain and suffering for the earth; karma is created that will have to be rectified in future planetary epochs. But the eagle and the cow do what man is unable to do: through its feathers the eagle takes spiritualized earth substance into the world of the spirit, and the cow gives materialized spiritual substance to the earth through its digestive processes. Initiation science lives in the inner response to such knowledge. Rejoicing of earth spirits in the activities of the cow, and of air and fire spirits in the activities of the eagle. Criticism of a statement made by Albert Schweitzer. The lion creates the right balance between eagle and cow.

Lecture 4, 26 October 1923

Recapitulation of the four stages of Earth evolution: Saturn (heat), Sun (air), Moon (water), Earth (solid). Distinction between the upper nature of the first two and the lower nature of the second two. Each stage of evolution leaves its effects in later stages, e.g. Moon forces left in the earth work in magnetism and gravity. The butterfly is a creation of the upper cosmic forces. Its egg is under direct influence of the sun, the caterpillar of Mars, the chrysalis of Jupiter, and the freed butterfly of the sun's light and Saturn forces. In Moon evolution the plant embryos came under the influence of Moon-Earth forces. The plant seed belongs to the earth, the leaf corresponds to the crawling caterpillar, the calyx to the cocoon, the flower to the freed butterfly. Influences of the lower planets—Moon, Venus, Mercury—supplant the upper planets which influence the butterfly. The butterfly is the freed plant, the plant the fettered butterfly. Their joy in each other. Artistic perception needed for true knowledge.

Lecture 5, 27 October 1923

Recapitulation. The butterfly continually gives spiritualized substance to the cosmos during life, birds only on death. Butterflies are creatures of light ether, birds of warmth. Warmed air penetrates bones of birds and makes up 'air bird'; a bird's physical body is merely its 'luggage'. The butterfly takes light-filled air into its body. Both bird and butterfly overcome gravity, but bats have marrow-filled bones and do not overcome it. Bats dislike light; their flight can be explained on the basis of earthly dynamics and mechanics. Butterflies see things of the earth as mirror of cosmos, birds see what lives in air, bats perceive things of the earth but are full of listening fear. Butterflies are memories, birds are thoughts, bats are dreams. Bats give off spiritualized substance as a kind of 'magma' in the air. People used to feel the need to defend themselves against this, for, inhaled by man, it becomes the food of the Dragon. The Michael impulse protects man today.

Lecture 6, 28 October 1923

Man has the longest evolution, beginning with the head on Saturn, when butterflies also began to evolve. Man develops inwardly, the butterfly outwardly. The chest developed on Sun with the lion, which added head and limbs later. The beginnings of limbs and digestive system came on Moon, with the cow, which later added chest and head. Amphibians and reptiles pure digestion animals. Fishes appeared when man developed reproductive organs. Butterflies and birds are a metamorphosed memory, in miniature, of the beings of the hierarchies man knew on Saturn and Sun. They were thus rightly used to depict spiritual beings. Man is called down into a new incarnation by the 'butterfly corona' shot through with rays from birds, i.e. head nature. Fishes do not feel themselves to be water creatures, but etheric creatures that envelop water. They are aware of the 'breathing' of the earth. The frog is connected with the astral of the earth and responds to weather conditions. The cosmos creates frogs, toads, snakes, etc. using the same forces that are active in human digestion. Relation of toads to colon. Study of the mineral kingdom will reveal the future as study of animals has revealed the past. Formation of minerals. The pineal body.

Lecture 7, 2 November 1923

Mystery of plant life. Gnomes, which work around roots, are sense organs with immediate intelligence. They despise human logic. Through the plant they gather the ideas of the cosmos while remaining connected with the earth. This threatens them with the danger of becoming frogs or toads. Undines or water spirits work in leaf development and in the moist air. They dream the chemistry of plant life. Their fear is to become fish. Sylphs live in warmth and air, especially in air movements caused by birds, which give them a feeling of ego. They bear cosmic love through the atmosphere and are also light-bearers, creating the archetypal plant forms out of light that later go down to the gnomes. Salamanders or fire spirits live in light and warmth which they carry to the pollen in the flowers which then takes it to the seed. All this is a male process. Fertilization occurs in winter when the seeds meet the ideal plant forms guarded by the gnomes. Goethe's instinctive feeling for this. Fire spirits feel their ego in connection with insects which actually live in their aura. Hence the power of butterflies to spiritualize matter. Gnomes and undines take gravity forces from the earth upwards to meet the light and warmth sent down by sylphs and fire spirits. Wonder of nature enhanced by spiritual science.

Lecture 8, 3 November 1923

Ancient powers of spiritual perception have withdrawn. Late evolved creatures have not developed the skeleton that evolved with the head principle; the gnomes are their spiritual complement. Gnomes create their bodies out of gravity; they are acutely attentive to the world. They are masked by images in our dreams. Undines support animals requiring a hard outer skeleton. They are hidden behind our dreamless sleep. Sylphs supply the limb system to birds. They lie behind our waking dreams. Fire spirits complement butterflies. Together with its fire spirit, the butterfly resembles a winged human being. Fire spirits are behind waking consciousness and thoughts. Malign gnomes and undines produce parasites. Relation of elimination to the brain. Malign sylphs produce plant poisons, e.g. deadly nightshade. Brahma, Vishnu, Shiva.

Lecture 9, 4 November 1923

For the gnomes the earth is a hollow space and offers no resistance. They experience the different qualities of its substances. Their relation to the moon, and their different appearance at its phases. Their work in carrying over what is good in the solid structure of the earth from one manifestation to another. Undines assimilate the colours of phosphorescent water and offer themselves to the hierarchies. The sylphs carry the astrality of dying birds to the hierarchies. The fire spirits do the same with the gleaming of the warmth ether on butterflies' wings. All four classes of elemental spirits are astonished at man's lack of awareness in sleep. They speak to man in admonishment. Their sayings, which are part of the creative Word.

Lecture 10, 9 November 1923

Origin of the different systems of man. Limb system from the Earth, metabolic system from the Moon, rhythmical system from the Sun, nerves and senses from Saturn. All substances taken into the body must be transformed: mineral into warmth ether, plant into air processes, animal into water processes. Only the purely human may be saved. Carbon created in man disperses ether, which penetrates the sense organs and opens man to spiritual influences. Metabolic processes would cause illness if they were not kept in check by healing processes born on Sun. Breathing has a cosmic rhythm and restrains the circulation rhythm. Comparison with Saturn. Joy of the first two hierarchies in this healing process. Man's spiritual activity in relation to healing. Inflammation caused by blood processes entering nerves; tumours by nerve processes entering the blood. Relation of education to health. World healing process in the function of metals. Human therapy a microcosm of world therapy.

Lecture 11, 10 November 1923

All food must be transformed in the human organism. Mineral substance is changed into warmth ether to receive forces for the building of the body. Children can only transform milk. Untransformed substance causes disease, e.g. diabetes. External temperatures also must not enter the body. What root and flower in the plant say to man. Roots laid down when moon was united with earth. Plant liberated when moon left earth. Earth-bound root and heaven-seeking flower reverse their position when the plant becomes an air-being in man. In digestion, pulses dull the powers of the head. Reversal of the plant cannot properly take place in animal digestion. Elemental spirits of fear run counter to the animal's satisfaction in digestion. Kamaloka of carnivorous animals. Anthroposophy never fanatical (e.g. in diet) but only shows the truth. Milk for children, honey for the old; beehive a head without a skull in outer nature. 'A land flowing with milk and honey'.

Lecture 12, 11 November 1923
Spiritual and moral swallowed up in convention today. Its true source is human love and understanding. Why do we see the opposite in life? Hatred and lack of understanding spring not from the spiritual but from the physical. Relation of bone to hatred and blood to lack of understanding and moral coldness. Terror in initiation in perceiving that the body is built of hatred and coldness; after death these are taken from us by the third and second hierarchies so that we may meet the first hierarchy at the 'midnight hour'. The human form dissolves from the head down, and a new spiritual form is created that will be the head in the next incarnation. Thinking with the limbs. Rhythmical and digestive organs by second and third hierarchies. Hatred necessary for structure of bones. Hatred and coldness not fully absorbed by human beings today become cancer in civilization. Waldorf education the antidote. The need to come awake in the sphere of culture.

Introduction

As I write these words, spring gathers strength in this part of the world at last. Now that the lambs' tails have shed their pollen, the hedgerow swells with a marvellously green geometry of growth. Every tender little plant presents its clarity of form and orders its own rhythm and tone comfortably within the generous scale of nature. Even the April rain, hardly fair after a year of sodden months, astounds with its elegance as it falls clean and spare, each slanted rod catching light from the sun. The countryside in spring has inspired artists of all kinds, and given poets the courage to declare an amiable, harmonious plan in nature, a well-regulated, intentional universe. Such thoughts, however, beg the question raised by other country scenes of which we in Britain have been particularly aware at the time of writing: news pictures, of heaped animal carcasses awaiting cremation or burial, bring home to us daily the tragedy of the thousands of victims of a rampant outbreak of foot and mouth disease.

Although this volume of lectures does not speak directly to the issue of animal health, nevertheless it helps to create a context within which all events of the natural world can be thought through intelligently, imaginatively and purposefully, establishing in this way a new basis for our treatment of the environment and the creatures in our care.

In the year 1923, when these lectures were given, Europe was in crisis. The economic disease of hyperinflation was demoralizing everyone, social disorder infected the streets and, in Germany, the first germs of National Socialism were beginning to spread. Social healing was desperately needed.

Rudolf Steiner, a scientist and social philosopher from Austria, had made strenuous efforts after the Great War to influence government leaders with his ideas on a new model for society. In this he was unsuccessful, but he continued to address social concerns more obliquely in many other areas of his work. During the post-war years he was deeply engaged in founding a new system of education, as well as a radical approach to medicine, agriculture and nutrition, religion and the arts. In each of these specialist fields he was able to indicate, from his own spiritual research, how a more comprehensive understanding of the human being in body, soul and spirit could lead to a new perspective on the world in general and human life and society in particular.

The lectures that follow were given to a non-specialized gathering, and are a sovereign example of what has come to be called 'holistic thinking', which for Steiner was the only way of thinking with any relevance at all for civilization. Readers will discover how many and detailed are the ways in which the human being can be seen as microcosm, and how all kingdoms of nature have been guided into being by the wise dynamics of the cosmos. Here is an inspirational scheme of the world as a living flux of spirit seeking incorporation into matter, and matter itself seeking to be spiritualized; here is a world picture which has as its genesis and goal the idea of the truly human being, whose evolution has been carried spiritually by the creativity of cosmic forces since the very beginning.

Before the war, in September 1912, Steiner was walking the foothills of the Jura mountains above a small village in Switzerland, close to Basle and the German and French borders. Swiss friends had offered him a piece of land, hoping that a building could be erected there to serve as a centre for the movement which became, in the following year, the Anthroposophical Society. As it turned out, the final decision to build near this modest village of Dornach and not in Germany was a particularly auspicious one in the light of the turbulent decades which were soon to overwhelm Europe. The foundation stone was laid on 20 September 1913.

The building was of unusual design, with a double dome and constructed almost entirely of wood. It was called the 'Goetheanum' in honour of the German luminary J. W. von Goethe, and lent its name to the periodical mentioned in these lectures. Sadly, this first building was lost in a fire on New Year's Eve 1922/23, before the finishing touches had been completed. Plans began immediately for rebuilding, and a new Goetheanum was dedicated at Christmas 1923 when, at the same time, the Anthroposophical Society was refounded. This second Goetheanum, shaped in steel-reinforced concrete and looking not unlike a craggy outcrop of the Jura, stands today on the Dornach hill, a busy centre of a worldwide Society, welcoming students, researchers and curious visitors from all over the globe.

So it came to be in the very down-to-earth setting of a makeshift lecture hall in a workshop on a building site that Steiner gave this cycle of twelve lectures, speaking on each Friday, Saturday and Sunday of four consecutive weekends in late autumn 1923. His listeners were all members of the Anthroposophical Society, which is why the lectures occasionally assume a familiarity with Steiner's work. Readers must also keep in mind that the content is unrevised by the author.

The weekly rhythm of delivery has shaped these lectures into four groups of three, each group opening a different window on the phenomena of the natural world. Part One introduces us straightaway to the theme of the whole course: that human beings reflect in every way the laws and the secrets of the world within which they live. We are offered something here that contrasts very strongly with modern theories of the human being as a late and possibly temporary visitor to planet Earth; humanity is portrayed as knitted firmly and forever into the whole fabric of existence.

Steiner is quick to establish ground rules for this study: we must exercise flexibility of mind, a thoughtful imagination which he encompasses with the phrase 'artistic perception'. He leads us through some examples of what he means and then, in case we begin to feel over-confident in the method, he sobers us with the task of transmogrifying in thought an eagle into a cow.

In exploring the ancient picture of the human being as a unity of Eagle, Lion and Bull, Steiner shows us how each of these three animal groups presents a certain temptation, and he modernizes an African fable to illustrate his points. For a long time I was mystified by this tale, but now I think that it is about our position in a world where awareness of a spiritual heritage has been destroyed by materialistic thinking. When a one-sided development of the intellect (hyena) recognizes only material reality, it will have to distance itself from the less substantial emotional life and shadowy world of unconscious motivations. Unacknowledged feelings (lion) and frustrated ideals (wolf) are thrown into confusion and they become self-seeking and mutually destructive. The intellect is left to grow fat on a decayed emotional life and a disintegrating capacity for initiative, and free to continue feeding on the physical matter (in effect the corpse) of the human being (antelope). Such fables are ever open to interpretation—so let us share our discoveries!

Throughout these lectures Steiner's deep concern with the future of medicine keeps coming to the surface. Is he fishing the audience for those who might take up the work? A few weeks previously he had been in England speaking to a group of physicians, later more doctors were gathered with him in Vienna and there would shortly be similar meetings in Holland. Meanwhile he maintained his regular visits as adviser to

a therapeutic clinic, founded by a colleague in the neigh-
bouring village of Arlesheim. The breadth of his notion of
healing becomes apparent as he describes the potential sickness of our planet, how it is caused by the very existence of
human life, and how healing is achieved through the animal
creation. He manages in every way to weave together earthly
observations and spiritual knowledge so that meaning and
purpose are brought once again into life.

Part Two of the lecture cycle continues to nourish our
understanding with artistic thoughts. We come to see the
butterfly first as a 'fluttering plant of the air', then as 'enduring
thoughts of memory'; birds become flying 'thoughts of the
moment' and the bat a 'flying dream picture of the cosmos'.
Keeping thought processes imaginative and flexible in this
way is of great help when it comes to following the meta-
morphic steps in evolution which are sketched somewhat
broadly in this section. Certain passages may appear difficult
to those who are unfamiliar with Steiner's book *An Outline of
Esoteric Science*, but they will reward patient study.

A piece on the ethers and the elements in Lecture 5 seems
to me to need a diagram for clarification. If Steiner had used
the blackboard at this juncture, I think he might have drawn
something like eight concentric circles and marked them from
the outside as 'life ether, chemical ether, light ether, cosmic
heat ether, earthly heat, air, water, earth', with an indication
that the two aspects of heat were continually interpenetrating.

The section ends with more examples of how 'World and
man belong together in every respect'. These words were
followed by a diagram (unfortunately only verbal) that was
intended for elucidation, but its description is still making
demands upon the brain of this writer.

The content of the third set of lectures concerns the astral-
etheric beings known as elemental spirits, whose existence is

rarely acknowledged today beyond the sphere of folklore. We discover how indebted we are to these beings, both ben-evolent and malevolent, for our continued existence. Steiner gives an account of their different levels of consciousness and, in doing so, throws light on some of the characters from tra-ditional nursery tales. Many of us will be familiar with the wise but gruff dwarf, the water sprite or mermaid who tries to lure the human being into its own fluid consciousness-world, and the unearthly beauty of the fairy queen which would entrap men and render them powerless, as if they slept. The fact that the elemental spirits, like irresponsible children, might choose to sport with the unprotected human consciousness should not undermine the fact that these spirits 'wish man to make a move onwards with his consciousness, so that he may be able to participate in their world'.

A series of meditative invocations from the nature spirits ends this section. If we would only listen in the right way, these might be heard sounding from just across the borders of our world. The words are redolent of the nature and endea-vour of each group, but also give warning to men and women to take stock of their situation and develop their conscious-ness. To utter these trenchant words for the benefit of man-kind is as important to the elemental world as any of its other work. But, as Steiner remarks: 'Whether or not man does perceive such things depends upon his own free choice.'

The final trio of the lecture cycle looks again at how our life in a body gradually evolved and continues to evolve. We learn how each particle of food has to be utterly transformed before it can build the human body; we discover that a subtle transformation of carbon occurs with the human breath, allowing the influence of helpful spiritual forces to build a foundation for our thinking. Steiner compares the bias to illness within the digestive system with the inclination to healing of the blood circulation, contending that such facts need to be assimilated by any really modern approach to the arts of both medicine and education. Pedagogy and medicine are seen as two sides of the same coin. The new Waldorf education movement was demanding a lot of Steiner's time both in Germany and abroad. The visit to England mentioned earlier had included an enthusiastic reception at a teachers' seminar in Ilkley, but it would be two more years before the first Waldorf School in London opened its doors.

The health of the human body, soul and spirit depends on nutrition being led into healing, from there into spiritual-cultural activity and back again to healing. Now we understand why a Waldorf teacher takes an interest in his pupils' circulation, and why the arts are renowned for their therapy. Less easy to understand is the story of the simple carrot which, when liberated from the shackles of earthly life, seeks out and penetrates the head organism and uses its activity as a springboard to the spiritual spaces it so longs for. In this extraordinary way, the human being becomes integrated into the evolutionary striving of the plant world.

References have been made earlier to Steiner's pre-occupation with social reform and in the last lecture he reaches the nub of all social issues: the presence or absence in society of mutual understanding and love. The lack of these he traces to a cause deep within our bodily foundation, for just as physical cold causes us to draw our body together, so it is the spiritual force of 'moral coldness' that is needed to contract our bones. 'It is good for our bones to have a certain hardness', however '. . . it is not good for our social life if our souls have this hardness.'

The description of mankind burdened with moral coldness stands in expressive contrast with the gracious understanding and loving care of the angelic beings who guide the soul on its transformative journey after death. The journeys of many souls through the spiritual world have created a superfluity of moral coldness which now invades the spiritual atmosphere of the earth and causes much malaise in modern life. The cure Steiner prescribes for this is the cultural pedagogy to be found in the Waldorf school method, but he fears that Central Europe might become so sick as to fight the cure. This concern was justified, for as Nazi power grew bolder so Waldorf schools were forced to close.

Rudolf Steiner died on 30 March 1925, and so did not live to see the closure of the schools, nor the subsequent spread of his educational methods to many far-flung regions of the world.

Steiner's work was much and varied. He was able to be at ease with professional people or blue-collar workers, with artists and intellectuals, always tailoring his style to the nature or the nationality of his audience. In these lectures we catch glimpses of the rich soul moods that coloured this remarkable personality. He communicates his delight in beauty and his reverential awe before the marvels of the spirit world; he shares his feelings of wonder for the majesty of creation and his sober witness of those spiritual facts which are more difficult to bear. With animated soul he offers these closing words: 'People are asleep. It is time, however, that we woke up.'

Nearly 80 years have passed and many *do* hear the groans of a creation whose harmony has been disturbed. But, as the smoking pyres of dead animals illustrate, there is still some way to go.

Ann Druitt
April 2001

Part One

Man's Connection with the Cosmos, the Earth and the Animal World

> 'We must be able to study the human being not merely by applying logic, but in a sense which can never be achieved unless intellectualism is taken onward into the artistic element in the world.'

Lecture 1

19 October 1923

It has often been said in our studies, and it has also been evident in the recent lectures on the four seasons and the archangels,* that in their form and structure, in the conditions of their life and indeed in every respect, human beings are a whole world, a microcosm as distinct from the macrocosm. All the laws and all the secrets of the world are to be found in them. This is of course an abstract way of putting it, and it will be far from easy to get at the real meaning of it. We'll need to enter into the many secrets of world and cosmos, and then see how we find them again in the essential human being.

Today we'll examine the world and then the human being from certain points of view, and we may then discover how the microcosm of the human being relates to the macrocosm. Anything we are able to say about the macrocosm can of course only refer to a small part of it. To present the whole of it, our studies would have to traverse the whole world.

Let us begin by considering what is immediately above us, the part of our environment where the animal kingdom lives in the air, and specifically the creatures that are most obviously living in the air—the birds.

It cannot escape us that the birds which live in the air,

---

* Rudolf Steiner. *The Four Seasons and the Archangels.* Five lectures given in Dornach just before this, on 5–13 October 1923. Rudolf Steiner Press, London 1996.

finding the essentials of life in the air, have quite a different form from animals that live either on or beneath the ground. Looking at a bird we will find, if we take the conventional view, that it too has a head, limbs, and so on. But that is a thoroughly inartistic way of looking at things. I have often drawn attention to the fact that, if we want to get to know the world, it will not be enough to grasp it with the intellect; we must develop an artistic way of seeing the world. If you do that, you certainly won't consider the 'head' of a bird—so dwarfed and stunted when compared to the heads of other animals—to be a head in the true sense. Yes, if you take an external, excessively intellectual view you may well say: 'That bird has a head, a body and limbs.' But just consider how poorly developed are the legs of a bird in comparison, let us say, with those of a camel or an elephant, and how dwarfed its head when compared to that of a lion or a dog. There is hardly anything worth speaking of in a bird's head; not much more, really, than would be the front part of the mouth in a dog or an elephant or a cat. I think it is fair to say that the bird's head is only slightly more elaborate than the front part of a mammal's mouth. As to the limbs of a mammal—they are completely atrophied in a bird. Certainly, if one takes an inartistic view one may talk of the forelegs of a bird as having been transformed into wings. But that is a thoroughly inartistic, unimaginative way of looking at things. If we really want to understand nature, really penetrate the cosmos, we must look more deeply—and above all to the powers that create and shape the things of this world.

The view that a bird, too, simply has a head, a body and limbs will never help us to get a true picture, for instance, of the bird's etheric body. If we use imaginative perception to advance from the physical to the etheric aspect, the bird will prove to be nothing but a head in its etheric aspect. The etheric bird is nothing but a head; and from this point of view it is immediately obvious that a bird cannot be compared to

the head, body and limbs of other animals, but must be
regarded simply and solely as a head, a transformed head. The
actual head of a bird represents merely the palate and front
parts of the head, i.e. the mouth parts; the parts of the bird's
skeleton that look like ribs and spine must be considered to be
head—though metamorphosed and transformed, it is true.
The whole bird is really head. The point is that, to understand
the bird, we must go a very long way back in the planetary
evolution of the Earth.*

Birds have a long planetary history, much longer than
camels, for example, which are of much later origin than any
bird. More earth-bound types of bird, such as the ostrich,
evolved later than those that have the freedom of the air—
eagles, vultures—which are very ancient creatures of the
earth. In earlier Earth, Moon and Sun epochs they certainly
still had everything which then, passing from within outwards
as far as the skin, later developed in birds of today into what
you see as feathers and a horny beak. The outer parts of birds
are of a later origin; this is due to the fact that birds developed
relatively early as head creatures. When they had to live under
the conditions that came later in Earth evolution the feathers
could only be added on the outside. The plumage was given
to birds by the Moon and the Earth; the rest of the bird comes
from much earlier epochs.

There is however a much deeper aspect to this. Let us look
at a bird in the air—an eagle, let us say, in its majestic flight.
Under the influence of the sun's rays it has received its plumage—rather like an outer gift of grace—and a horny beak;
I'll come to the other effects of the sun's rays later. Let us

---

* For the basics of planetary earth evolution, see Rudolf Steiner's essays in
Cosmic Memory. Rudolf Steiner Publications, New York 1971; and his book
Occult Science. An Outline. Rudolf Steiner Press, London 1979. Recently
republished as *An Outline of Esoteric Science*. Anthroposophic Press, New
York 1997.

look at the eagle as it flies in the air. It is subject to certain forces. The sun does not merely have the physical powers of light and heat that we normally speak of. When I spoke before of the Druid Mysteries,* I drew your attention to the fact that the sun also has non-physical powers. These are what we must consider. They give the different species of birds their rich and varied colours and specific form of plumage. When we penetrate the nature of the sun's action with spiritual perception, we come to see why the eagle has its particular plumage. We must then enter deeply into eagle nature and develop an inner, artistic feeling for it and for the spiritual element within it; we need to perceive how sun impulses, that are further enhanced by others which I shall mention later, how sun impulses wash over the eagle, as it were, even before it emerges from the egg, and conjure out the feathers or, to be more exact, conjure them into its fleshy form. Only then may we ask ourselves: What significance does this have for us as human beings? The significance is that this is the same principle that makes the human brain the vehicle for thought. And you have the right insight into the macrocosm, into the great world of nature, if you are able to look at an eagle and say: The eagle has his plumage, his many-coloured feathers; the power that is active in them is also active in me and makes my brain the vehicle for thoughts. The power that creates the convolutions of the human brain and enables it to take up the inner salt force that provides the basis for the faculty of thought also gives the eagle in the air its feathers. Thus we become aware of a relationship to our thinking, aware of the human equivalent to the eagle's feathers in us. Our thoughts flow from the

---

* Lecture given in Dornach on 19 September 1923, 'The Sun Initiation of the Druid Priest and His Moon Science', published in *Man in the Past, the Present and the Future*. Rudolf Steiner Press, London 1982.

brain in the same way as the feathers stream out from the eagle.*

When we progress from the physical to the astral level, something of a paradox arises: on the physical plane those powers cause feathers to develop; on the astral plane they give rise to thoughts. Feathers are given to the eagle; that is the physical aspect of the process in which thoughts are formed. The thoughts given to human beings are the astral aspect of the development of feathers. Such things are sometimes indicated in a wonderful way through the genius of the vernacular, of common sayings. If a feather is cut off at the top and the contents are extracted, the country people in some German-speaking regions call this the 'soul'. Some people will no doubt take this to be simply an outer term, but it is not. Anyone who understands these things will find that a feather holds something tremendous: it holds the secret of how thoughts are formed.

Let us now turn away from the eagle that lives in the air, and consider a mammal, taking the lion as a representative example. The lion can really only be understood if we develop a feeling for the joy, the inner satisfaction, that lions have in living together with their whole environment. There is really no other animal, except for those related to the lion, which has such a wonderful, mysterious breathing process. In all animal nature, the breathing rhythms must harmonize with the rhythms of the blood circulation; the two rhythms differ in that the rhythms of the circulation grow heavy because of the digestive system that is tied up with them, and the breathing rhythms grow light in the endeavour to achieve the near weightless state of the physical brain. In birds, anything that lives in their breathing really lives at the same time in the head. A bird is all head and in a way outwardly represents the head

---

* Homer compares the speed of the Phoenician ships to a 'bird's wing or a thought'. *Odyssey* VII.36.—Ed.

in the world. Its thoughts are in its plumage. For anyone with a real feeling for the beauties of nature, there is hardly anything more moving than to experience the inner connection between human thought—when it is really concrete, inwardly teeming with life—and the plumage of a bird. Anyone who is inwardly practised in such things knows exactly when he is thinking like a peacock, when he is thinking like an eagle, or when he is thinking like a sparrow. Apart from the fact that the one is astral and the other physical, these things do actually correspond in a wonderful way. Those are the facts. And it may be said that breathing predominates to such an extent in a bird's life that other processes—the circulation and so on—are almost negligible. All the heaviness of digestion that imposes itself on the circulation is completely removed, done away with by the sense of itself in itself that the bird has.

In the lion a kind of balance exists between breathing and circulation. The lion's circulation is certainly also weighed down, but not as much as a camel's, for instance, or a cow's. In them the digestion burdens the circulation to a tremendous degree. In the lion, whose digestive tract is comparatively short and is made in such a way that the digestive process is completed as rapidly as possible, digestion does not burden the circulation to any marked degree. On the other hand, the head principle has developed in such a way in the lion's head that breathing is held in balance with the rhythm of circulation. In lions, more than in any other animal, the inner rhythms of breathing and heartbeat are in inner balance and harmony. This is why lions—if we enter into what may be called their subjective life—have that particular way of devouring their food with unbridled voracity, literally gulping it down. They are simply glad to have got it down. They are ravenous for nourishment because it is part of their nature that hunger causes them much more pain than it causes other animals. They are greedy for nourishment but they are not bent on being fastidious gourmets! They are not at all interested in taste sensation, for they are animals that find their inner satisfaction in the even rhythms of their breathing and circulation. It is only when the food has passed over into the blood which regulates the heartbeat, and when the heartbeat has come into reciprocal action with the breathing—it is a source of enjoyment to lions to draw breath and gives them deep inner satisfaction—it is only when they feel in themselves the result of their feeding, an inner balance between breathing and circulation, that lions are really in their element. They are wholly lion when they experience the deep inner satisfaction of the blood beating upwards and of the breath pulsing downwards. Lions are alive and in their element when these two wave movements come together.

Look at a lion, how it runs, how it leaps, how the head is held, even the look in its eye, and you will see that all this arises from a continuous rhythmical interplay between getting out of balance, and restoring balance again. Hardly anything else strikes us as more mysterious than the remarkable look in a lion's eye; so much is revealed there of inward mastery, the mastering of opposing forces. That is what we perceive in the look in a lion's eye: the heartbeat controlled by the breathing rhythm.

And again, let those who have an artistic eye for form look at the shape of the lion's mouth; this shows how the heartbeat pulses upwards as far as the mouth, but is held back by the breath. If you could really picture the way the heartbeat and breathing come in touch with each other, you would arrive at the shape of the lion's mouth.

The lion is all chest. In this animal the rhythmical system comes to perfect expression both in the outer form and in the way of life. Lions are organized in such a way that the interplay between heartbeat and breathing also comes to expression in the reciprocal relationship of heart and lungs.

We really have to say therefore that if we look for what most closely resembles the bird in the human being, in metamorphosed form, of course, we come to the human head; if we look for what most closely resembles the lion, it is the region of the human chest, where the rhythms of circulation and breathing meet.

Let us now turn our attention away from everything we perceive as the bird kingdom up there in the air, and from everything that lives in the circulation of the air in the immediate environment of the earth, for example in the lion. Let us consider the ox or cow. I have frequently spoken of the pleasure to be gained from watching a herd of cattle, lying replete and satisfied in a meadow, and from observing the process of digestion which here again comes to expression in the position of the body, in the expression of the eyes, in every movement. Make the opportunity to observe a cow lying in the meadow and its reaction when a noise comes from one direction or another. It is really marvellous to see how the animal raises its head, how in this lifting there lies the feeling that it is all heaviness, that it is not easy for a cow to lift its head, and there is something rather special going on. Seeing a cow in the meadow disturbed in this way, we cannot but say to ourselves: This cow is amazed at having to raise its head for anything but grazing. 'Why am I raising my head? I am not grazing, and there is no point in lifting my head unless it is to graze.' Just look at the way it happens. That is what goes on when a cow lifts its head. But it is not limited to the movement of the head. You cannot imagine a lion lifting its head the way the cow does. This lies in the shape of the head. And if we further observe the animal's whole form, we see that it is in fact what I may call a complete and utter digestive system! The weight of the digestion burdens the circulation to such a degree that it overwhelms everything to do with the head and breathing. The animal is all digestion. It is truly marvellous, if one looks with the eye of the spirit, to turn one's gaze upwards to the birds, and then downwards to the cow.

Of course, you can lift a cow as high as you like, it will never be a bird; but if one could at the same time let the physical aspect of the cow be transformed into a form of air and moisture—first taking it up into the moist air that is in the immediate vicinity of the earth and transforming the etheric configuration into one appropriate to the realm of moisture, and then raising the creature up higher and taking it as far as the astral, then the cow would be a bird up there in the heights. Astrally it would be a bird.

And you see, it is just here that a marvellous insight is gained and we say to ourselves: What the bird up in the heights has by way of astrality, through its astral body, that is working, as I have said, to form the plumage, is something the cow has taken into flesh, muscle and bone. Something that is astral in the bird has become physical in the cow. It does of course look different at the astral level, but this is so nevertheless.

On the other hand, if I reversed the process and allowed the bird's astrality to drop down, at the same time bringing about a transformation into the etheric and physical, the eagle would turn into a cow, because the astral element in the eagle is made flesh, a physical body, in the animal that lies on the ground when engaged in digestion. It is part of this digestive process in the cow to develop a wonderful astrality. The cow becomes beautiful in the process of digestion. Seen in its astral aspect, this digestive process has something infinitely beautiful. In the light of ordinary mundane notions, philistine ideas of perfection, the business of digestion is the lowest of the low. Yet one is proved utterly wrong in this once a higher point of view is achieved and one sees the digestive process in the cow with the eye of the spirit. It is beautiful, it is magnificent, it is something of a tremendously spiritual nature.

The lion does not attain to this spirituality, much less the bird. In the bird the digestive process is something almost entirely physical. One does of course find the etheric body in the digestive system of the bird, but there is very little astrality, almost none. Compared to this the digestive processes of the cow are in astral terms quite stupendous, an entire world.

If we now want to look for similar things in the human being, for something corresponding to what in the cow is a one-sided development, the physical embodiment of a certain astral element, we find it in the human digestive organs and their continuation in the limbs—harmoniously interwoven with what else is there. The things I see in the eagle high in the air above me, and in the animal that rejoices in the air around him the way the lion does, and in the animal connected with earth forces that come from below ground and are active also in the digestive organs—that is, if I look not up to the heights, but down into the depths, entering into the nature of the cow with real understanding—I find all three configurations united into one, harmonized and balanced in the human being. I find the metamorphosis of the bird in the human head, the metamorphosis of the lion in the human chest, and the metamorphosis of the cow in the digestive system and the limbs—once again utterly metamorphosed, utterly transformed.

If today we contemplate these things and realize again that man is actually born out of the whole of nature, that he bears the whole of nature within him, as I have shown, that he bears the bird kingdom, the lion kingdom, the essential nature of the cow in him, then we have the individual aspects of what is expressed in the abstract sentence: Man is a microcosm. He is indeed a microcosm, and the macrocosm is in him; and all the creatures that live in the air, all the animals on the face of the earth whose special element is the air that circulates there, and the animals whose special element is below the surface of the earth, in the forces of gravity—all these work together in man as a harmonious whole. So that man is synthesis of eagle, lion, and ox or cow.

When these things are researched and rediscovered through a modern science of the invisible, of the spirit, one gains that great respect for old instinctive clairvoyant insight into the cosmos of which I have often spoken, respect for the mighty vision that man consists of eagle, lion, and cow or ox which, harmonized in true proportion, together form the human being in his wholeness.

But before I go on—this may be tomorrow—to discuss the separate impulses, for example, that are active in the forces streaming around the eagle, around the lion, around the cow, I want to speak of another correspondence between man's inner being and what is outside in the cosmos.

What we have learned so far can lead us to this. When the human head looks for what accords with its nature it must direct its gaze upwards to the bird kingdom. The human chest—the heartbeat, the breathing—must, if it desires to grasp itself as one of the secrets of nature, turn its gaze to such a thing as the nature of the lion. And man must try to understand his metabolic system from the constitution, from the organization, of the ox or cow. But in his head man has the vehicle for his thoughts, in the chest the vehicle for his feelings, and in his metabolic system the vehicle for the will. So that in his soul-nature, too, man is an image of the thoughts that move through the world with the birds and find expression in their plumage; of the world of feeling that encircles the earth, which is to be found in the lion in the balanced life of heartbeat and breathing. These latter are toned down in man but still represent the quality of inner courage. An ancient Greek had the term $\epsilon\nu\psi\chi\iota\alpha$—'to be of good courage'—for these qualities of heart and chest.* And if man wishes to find the will impulses that are predominantly connected with the metabolism, to give them outer form, he looks to what has become flesh in the cow.

Something that may sound grotesque or paradoxical today

* Homer. See also Matthew 14,27: 'Take heart'. Also the quality of the 'great soul', cf. Coeur de Lion.—Ed.

and seem almost insane in an age when there is no longer any real understanding for the spiritual connections in the world, nevertheless contains a kernel of truth that goes back to ancient traditions. Mahatma Gandhi—he has now been presented to the world in somewhat rough and ready fashion in a pretty awful book by Romain Rolland*—is a man who certainly directs his activities entirely to outer affairs but at the same represents something like an eighteenth-century rationalist among the Indian people and in terms of the ancient Hindu religion. The remarkable phenomenon is that he has nevertheless actually retained the veneration of the cow in his enlightened Hinduism. This cannot be set aside, says Mahatma Gandhi, who, as you know, was sentenced to six years' imprisonment by the British for his political activities in India. He still retains the veneration of the cow.

Things such as these, which have so tenaciously persisted in more spiritual cultures, can only be understood when one is aware of the inner connections, when one really knows the tremendous secrets that lie in the ruminating animal, in the cow. Then we can understand why people come to venerate in the cow a sublime astrality that has, as it were, become earthly, and only in this respect more lowly. Such things enable us to understand the religious veneration paid to the cow in Hinduism, while the whole bevy of rationalistic and intellectualistic concepts which have been brought to bear on this subject will never enable us to understand it.

And so we see how will, feeling and thought can be looked for outside in the cosmos, and correspondingly in the microcosm of the human being.

There are, however, all kinds of other forces in the human being and outside in the world of nature too. I would ask you to take particular note of the following. Consider the meta-

---

* A biography translated from the original French and published in German in 1923.

morphoses undergone by the creature which finally becomes a butterfly.

As you know, the butterfly lays its egg and from that egg a caterpillar emerges. The egg completely encloses and contains everything that later gives rise to the butterfly. The caterpillar emerges from the egg into light-irradiated air. That is the environment into which the caterpillar comes. The important thing is to note that the caterpillar really lives in the sunlit air.

This is something you should study when you are lying in bed at night and have lit the lamp, and a moth flies towards the lamp and finds its death in the light. The effect of the light on the moth is such that it accepts that it has to seek its death. There you see how light acts on something that lives.

The caterpillar—I am only referring to this briefly today; tomorrow and the next day we'll go into more detail—cannot reach the source of light, which is the sun, in order to cast itself into it, but would like to do so. It wants it just as much as the moth does which casts itself into the flame of your bedside candle and there meets its death in a physical fire. The caterpillar seeks the flame just as eagerly, the flame which comes towards it from the sun. But it cannot throw itself into the sun; so its passage into heat, into light, is therefore a spiritual act for the caterpillar. The whole of the sun's action passes to the caterpillar as a spiritual activity. It follows every single sunbeam, this caterpillar; by day it follows the sunbeams. The moth casts itself into the flame in one moment, giving the whole of its moth substance over to the light; the caterpillar gradually weaves its caterpillar substance into the light, pauses at night, weaves by day, and spins and weaves a whole cocoon around itself. The cocoon, the threads of the cocoon, are what the caterpillar weaves out of its own substance as it spins on in the flood of sunlight. And so the caterpillar, once it has become a chrysalis, has woven around itself, out of its own substance, the sunbeams to which it has merely given physical substance. The moth is consumed quickly in the physical fire. The caterpillar, sacrificing itself, casts itself into the sunlight, and weaves around itself the threads of the sunbeams, following the direction in which they go at any given moment. If you look at a silkworm cocoon you are looking at woven sunlight, but sunlight given physical form from the substance of the silk-spinning caterpillar itself. The result is an enclosed inner space, so that outer sunlight has in a sense been overcome. You'll remember that when I described the Druid Mysteries I spoke of the sunlight which enters the cromlechs becoming inward. The sun, which previously exerted its physical power, causing the caterpillar to spin its own cocoon, now exerts power on what is inward, and out of this inner nature creates the butterfly, which then emerges. Then the whole cycle begins again. Here you have spread out before you in sequence what is contracted in a bird's egg.

Compare the whole process with what happens when a bird lays its eggs. Inside the bird itself, in a process that has undergone metamorphosis, a chalky eggshell develops around the egg.

The forces of the sunlight make use of the substance of the calcium carbonate to bring together in one process what is a whole sequence of egg, caterpillar and cocoon in the case of the butterfly. With processes that otherwise are separated into different stages thus brought together, the whole of the bird's embryonic development is different. In the bird, the first three stages are one whereas in the butterfly we have the separate, outwardly visible stages of egg, caterpillar and chrysalis/ cocoon, with the butterfly finally emerging.

Now what do we see if we follow the whole process at the astral level? The bird's whole form represents a human head, the organ where thoughts are evolved. What does the butterfly represent? It, too, lives in the airy element, but its embryonic development is a great deal more complex. It becomes apparent that the butterfly represents a continuation of the head function, it represents the forces of the head extended, as it were, to the whole human being. Something happens in the human being which corresponds to a different process in nature from that of bird development.

If we include the etheric and astral elements, the human head can be seen to have one function that is very similar to the one in which an egg is produced, except that it has been metamorphosed. However, if we only had this one function our thoughts would all be momentary. They would no longer go down inside us, involve the whole human being and then rise up again as memories. If I look at the momentary thoughts which I have in response to the outside world and then look up to the eagle, I say: In the eagle's feathers I see thoughts that outside myself have taken physical form; in me, they are thoughts, but only momentary thoughts. If I look to what I bear in me as my memories, I find a more complicated process. Down below in the physical body, a process similar to the development of an egg occurs, though in the etheric it is something quite different—an inner process similar to the outer development of the caterpillar; in the astral body it bears an inner resemblance to the development of a chrysalis, a cocoon. The process in which I perceive something that triggers a thought, which is pushed down, is similar to the way in which a butterfly lays its egg. The process of transformation is similar to what happens in the case of the caterpillar: the life in the etheric body offers itself to the light of the spirit, weaves an inner astral cocoon, as it were, around the thought, and the memories emerge from this. If we see the bird's plumage in our momentary thoughts, we must see the butterfly's wing, shimmering with colour, as something that at the spiritual level evolves in our remembered thoughts.

Thus we look around us and feel to what an immense degree nature is related to us. We think and we see the world of thoughts in the flying birds. We remember, we have memories, and see the world of memory images that live in us in the fluttering butterflies shimmering in the sunlight. Yes, man is a microcosm, and contains within himself the secrets of the macrocosm. And it is indeed true that the things we perceive inwardly—our thoughts, feelings, will impulses and memory pictures—seen from the other side, outside in the macrocosm, can be found again in the realm of nature.

That is what it means to look at reality. Reality of this kind cannot be grasped by mere thoughts, for to them reality is a matter of indifference. Only logic counts where they are concerned. But this same logic can be used to prove almost anything and everything in the real world. Let me close by giving you an example of this, giving you a picture that will form a bridge to what we will be considering tomorrow.

An African tribe, the Felatas, have a very beautiful fable, from which much can be learned.

Once upon a time a lion, a wolf and a hyena set out on a journey. They met an antelope. The antelope was torn to pieces by one of the animals. The three travellers were good friends, and now the question arose as to how they should divide the dismembered antelope between them. First the lion said to the hyena, 'You divide it.'

The hyena had its own logic. It is an animal that deals not with the living but with the dead. Its logic is no doubt determined by the measure of its courage, or rather lack of courage. Depending on this, it approaches reality in one way or another.

The hyena said, 'We'll divide the antelope into three equal parts—one for the lion, one for the wolf, and one for myself.' Then the lion fell upon the hyena and killed it. That was the end of the hyena. The antelope still had to be shared out. So the lion said to the wolf, 'Look here, my dear wolf, we'll have to share it out differently now. You divide it. How would you share it out?' Then the wolf said, 'Yes, we must now apportion it differently; there can't be equal shares, like before. Since you have rid us of the hyena, you as the lion must of course have the first third; the second would have been yours in any case, as the hyena said, and the remaining third shall be yours because you are the wisest and bravest of all animals.' That is how the wolf apportioned it. Then said the lion, 'Who taught you to divide in this way?' To which the wolf replied, 'The hyena taught me.'

So the lion did not devour the wolf, but, according to the wolf's logic, took all three portions for himself.

The mathematics, the intellectual element, was the same with the hyena and the wolf. Each divided the antelope into three parts. But they differed in the way they applied this to reality and that meant a major difference also in their destiny. The hyena was devoured because its application of the principle of division to reality had different results from that of the wolf. The wolf was not devoured because it applied hyena logic—it freely admitted that it had been taught by the hyena—to quite another reality. It applied it to reality in such a way that the lion no longer felt compelled to devour it.

So you get first of all hyena logic, and then hyena logic also in the wolf; but the intellectual logical element becomes something quite different when applied to reality.

That is how it is with all abstractions. You can do anything you like with abstractions, applying them to reality in one way or another. It is important, therefore, that we are able to see reality in the correspondence between man, as microcosm, and the macrocosm. We must be able to study the human being not merely by applying logic, but in a sense which can never be achieved unless intellectualism is taken onward into the artistic element in the world. If you succeed in bringing about the metamorphosis of intellectualism into artistic perception, and are able to develop this artistic approach into an instrument of perception, you will find in the outer macrocosm the phenomena that exist in the human being, though transformed there from how they manifest in the natural world. Then you will find that man is related to the macrocosm in a very true and real sense.

Lecture 2

20 October 1923

Having considered in the lecture yesterday the nature of the animals of the heights, represented by the eagle, the animals of the middle region, represented by the lion, and the animals of the earth's depths, represented by the ox or cow, we can today turn our attention to man's connection with the universe—to the particular aspect which shows how the inner organization of the human being relates to these representatives of the animal world.

Let us first turn our gaze to the regions of which we said yesterday that when the animal derives its particular forces from them, they really cause the whole animal to become head organization. There we see how the bird owes its very nature to the sun-irradiated atmosphere. This sun illumined atmosphere is a necessity, for the bird receives from it everything, we might say, that it is able to receive by virtue of the fact that it owes its essential existence to this atmosphere. And I told you yesterday that it is on this that the actual formation of plumage depends. The essential nature of the animal lies in its external features, as it were. What the outside world makes of it is embodied in its plumage. But when the influence of the sun-irradiated air is not impressed on the creature from without, as in the case of the eagle, but is activated within, as in the case of the human nervous system, then thoughts arise—momentary thoughts, as I said, thoughts of the immediate present.

When we thus turn our gaze, weighed down one could say

by all that results from such contemplation, upwards to the heights, it is to the tranquil atmosphere and to the streaming sunlight that our attention is drawn. We must not, however, think of the sun in isolation. The sun maintains its power through the fact that it comes into connection with the different regions of the universe. Human perception of these connections has resulted in relating the sun's activities with what is known as the zodiac, so that when the sunlight reaches the earth from Leo, from Libra or from Scorpio, this always means something different. It also means something different for the earth if the sun's light is strengthened or weakened by the other planets of our planetary system. And here different relationships arise in regard to the different planets; the relationships to the 'outer planets'—Mars, Jupiter and Saturn—are different from those to the 'inner planets'—Mercury, Venus and Moon.

If we now consider the organization of the eagle, it is most important first of all to observe how far the sun forces are modified, strengthened or weakened by their interaction with Saturn, Jupiter and Mars. It is not for nothing that legend speaks of the eagle as the bird of Jupiter. In general Jupiter is considered to be representative of the outer planets. And if we were to draw a diagram illustrating what is meant here, we would have to draw the sphere which Saturn has in the cosmos, and also those of Jupiter and Mars.

Let us draw this, so that we may actually see it, in a diagram: the Saturn sphere, the Jupiter sphere, the Mars sphere; we then show the transition to the sun sphere, giving us in the outermost part of our planetary system the interaction of sun, Mars, Jupiter, Saturn.

And when we see the eagle circling in the air we do in fact utter a reality when we say: The forces that stream through the air from the sun in such a way that they are composed of the interaction of the sun with Mars, Jupiter and Saturn—are the forces that live in the whole configuration, in the essential

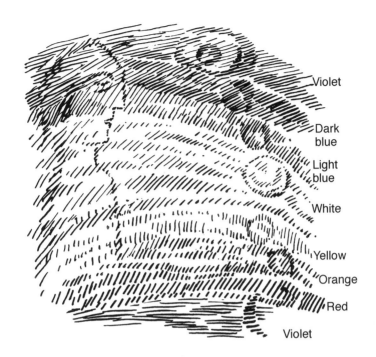

Violet

Dark
blue

Light
blue

White

Yellow

Orange

Red

Violet

nature of the eagle. But at the same time they live in the form
that has arisen as the human head. And when we place man in
the universe in accordance with his true reality—on earth he is
only, so to speak, a miniature image of himself—we must
place him in the eagle sphere as regards his head.

We must, therefore, think of the human being in regard to
his head as belonging to the eagle sphere; this is the aspect of
the human being that is connected with the forces in the upper
sphere.

The lion is the representative of the animals which are in the
real sense sun animals, in which the sun unfolds its own
special force. The lion prospers best when the planets above
the sun and the planets below the sun* are in a constellation
where they exert the least influence on the sun itself. Then

---

*Presumably so-called 'superior' and 'inferior' planets.—Ed.

those special characteristics appear which I described to you yesterday, namely, that the forces of the sun itself, penetrating the air, produce in the lion a breathing system of just such a kind that its rhythm is in perfect balance with the rhythm of the circulation, not in a numerical sense but as regards its dynamics. In the lion this balances itself out in a wonderfully beautiful way. The lion regulates its circulation through the breathing, and the circulation continually stimulates the stream of the breath. I told you that this can be seen even in the form, in the very shape of the lion's mouth. In this form the wonderful relationship between the rhythm of the blood and the rhythm of the breath is actually expressed. One can see this, too, in the remarkable gaze of the lion, resting in itself, and yet looking boldly outwards.

But what lives in the lion's gaze lives also in the organization of the human chest and heart, in the rhythmical organization which connects with the other elements of human nature— the metabolic system and the head system.

And if we picture unconstrained sun activity we must put the human being into the diagram in such a way that we place his heart and lungs in the region of this sun activity. It is here, in this sphere, that we have the lion nature in man.

When we turn to the inner planets nearer the earth, the 'inferior' planets, we have first the Mercury sphere. This has to do in particular with the finer parts of the metabolic system or organism of man, the region where foodstuffs are transformed into lymph-like substance and then taken over into circulation of the blood.

Progressing further, we come into the region of Venus activity. This is connected with the somewhat coarser parts of man's metabolic system, to that part of the human organism which works primarily from the stomach on the foodstuffs which have been consumed. We next come to the sphere of the moon. (I am drawing this in the sequence customary today in astronomy; I could also draw it differently.) There we enter the region which exerts influence on the metabolic processes, for these are connected with the moon.

In this way we have placed man within the entire universe. By turning our minds to the cosmic activities which the sun carries out in conjunction with Mercury, Venus and moon, we come to the region containing forces which are taken up by the order of animals represented for us by the cow, in the sense which I spoke of yesterday. There we have what the sun cannot do by itself alone, but what it can only do when its own forces are conducted to the earth by means of the planets nearest to the earth. When these forces are all at work, when they do not only stream through the air, but penetrate the earth's surface in various ways, then they work upwards from the earth's depths. And what thus works from the depths belongs to the sphere which we see embodied outwardly in the organism of the cow.

The cow is the animal of digestion. It is, moreover, the animal which accomplishes digestion in such a way that there lies in its digestive processes the earthly reflection of something actually super-earthly; its whole digestive process is permeated with an astrality which reflects the entire cosmos in a wonderful, light-filled way. There is—as I said yesterday—a whole world in this astral organism of the cow, but everything is based on gravity, everything is so organized that the earth's gravity works there. You have only to consider that a cow is obliged to consume about an eighth of its weight in food each day. Man can be satisfied with a fortieth part and remain healthy. Thus the cow needs earth's gravity in order to fully meet the needs of its organism. This organism is designed for the gravity of matter. Every day the cow must metabolize an eighth of her weight. This binds the cow with its material substance to the earth; yet through its astrality it is at the same time an image of the heights, of the cosmos.

This is why, as I said yesterday, the cow is an object of so much veneration for those who follow the Hindu religion. The Hindu says to himself: The cow lives here on the earth; but through this fact it creates in physical matter, subject to gravity, an image of something super-earthly.

It is indeed the case that man's nature is organized in a normal way when harmony is established between these three cosmic activities, which manifest in a one-sided way in eagle, lion and cow; when the human being is the confluence of the activities of eagle, lion and cow, or bull.

In accordance with the general course of world events, however, we are now living in an age when the evolution of the world is threatened by a certain danger; and this danger will be—if I may so express myself—that those one-sided influences actually come to one-sided expression in human beings. From the fourteenth and fifteenth centuries up to our own day the facts of human earthly evolution are such that, to an ever increasing degree, eagle forces wish to concentrate one-sidedly on the human head, lion forces on the human rhythmic system, and cow forces on the human metabolism and all human activity on earth.

This is the stamp of our age, that it is the aim of the cosmic powers to bring about a threefold division of man, and that each form of these cosmic powers is always striving to suppress the others. The eagle strives to subjugate the lion and the cow and make them of no account, and in like manner with each of the other elements. In our present age something particularly alluring is working on the subconscious in man; alluring because in a certain sense there is also something beautiful about it. In his conscious life man today is unaware of this, but in his subconscious, three calls surge and sound through the world, seeking to tempt him with their allurement. And I must say that it is the secret of our present time that from the sphere of the eagle there sounds down to man what actually gives the eagle his eagle nature, what gives it its plumage, what hovers around it as astrality. It is the eagle nature itself which becomes audible for the subconscious of man. This is the alluring call:

Learn to know my nature!
I give you the power
To create a universe
In your own head.

Thus speaks the eagle. That is the call from above, which today wishes to impose one-sidedness on man.

And there is a second alluring call. This is the call which comes to us from the middle region where the forces of the cosmos form the lion nature and where through the mingling of the sun and air they bring about equilibrium between the rhythms of breathing and circulation that constitutes the nature of the lion. What thus vibrates through the air, from the nature of the lion, what wills to make man's own rhythmic system one-sided, speaks alluringly to man's subconsciousness, saying:

Learn to know my nature!
I give you the power
To embody the universe
In the radiance of encircling air.

Thus speaks the lion. These voices which speak to man's subconscious have more effect than is supposed. Yes, my dear friends, human beings on earth are organized in different ways on earth. For instance, everyone who lives in the West is specially prone to be allured, to be led astray, by the voice of the eagle. Thus American civilization, on account of the special organization of its people, is particularly exposed to the temptation offered by what the eagle speaks. And Central Europe, which is imbued with much of the culture of classical antiquity, contains so much of what moved Goethe, for instance, to make his Italian journey, a journey which acted on his life like a liberation. Central Europe is particularly exposed to what is uttered by the lion.

Oriental civilization is pre-eminently exposed to what is uttered by the cow. And just as the other two animals give utterance in their cosmic representation, so there sounds upwards from the depths, like a rumbling, muffled roar, the call of what lies in the heaviness of the cow. It is truly the way I described to you yesterday, that when one sees a herd of cattle replete with grazing, sees them as they lie there in their own peculiar way, their very form revealing that they are given over to earth's gravity, all this is conditioned by the fact that this bodily form must daily metabolize an eighth of its own weight. And to this must be added that the depths of the earth, which under the influence of the sun, Mercury, Venus and the moon bring all this about in the digestive system of the cow—that these depths, as if with demonic rumbling power, resound through such a herd with the words:

> Learn to know my nature!
> I give you the power
> To wrest from the universe
> Measure, number and weight.

Thus speaks the cow. And it is the Orient which is especially exposed to the allurement of this call. But though the Orient is primarily exposed to this alluring call of the cow on account of the ancient veneration of the cow in Hinduism, if this allurement were actually to seize hold of mankind so that what arises from it gained mastery, then the influences emanating from the Orient would produce a civilization which, spreading through Central Europe and the West, would hinder progress and give rise to decadence. The demonic earth-forces would work on earth civilization in a one-sided way. What then would actually happen?

The following would happen. In the course of the last centuries, technology, an outer life of technology, has developed under the influence of external science. Certainly our technical progress is wonderful in every sphere. The forces of nature are active in technology in their lifeless form. And the important factors in bringing these lifeless forces into play so absolutely and utterly that they come to inform civilization throughout the earth—these factors are number, measure and weight.

The scales, the measuring rod—to weigh, to count, to measure—these are the ideal of the modern scientist, of the modern technician, whose entire profession has actually developed on the basis of external science. We have brought things to such a pass that an important mathematician of our times, in response to the question 'What is the guarantee of existence?' gave the following answer. (Philosophers of all ages have tried to answer the question of what is actually real.) This important physicist said: 'Anything that can be measured is real; anything that cannot be measured is not real.' The ideal thing, in this view, is for everything that exists to be brought into the laboratory, and weighed, measured and counted. From the results of this weighing, measuring and counting, one construes the things that are accepted as science, which then informs technology. Number, measure and weight are therefore meant to become the foundation of all civilization.

Now as long as people only use their ordinary understanding to apply measure, number and weight, things are not particularly bad. People are certainly clever, but they are still a long way from being as clever as the universe. And this is why things cannot become particularly bad so long as, in comparison with the universe, they go about their measuring, weighing and counting in a dilettante way. But if present-day civilization were to be transformed into initiation, things would be bad indeed if this attitude of mind remained. And this could happen if the civilization of the West, which stands entirely under the sign of measure, number and weight, were to be flooded by what might well come to pass in the East, namely, that through initiation science people might fathom what actually lives spiritually in the organism of the cow. For if you were to penetrate into the organism of the cow, burdened with earthly heaviness, with this eighth of its weight in foodstuffs, with all that can be weighed, measured and counted, if you were to learn what is being organized spiritually in the cow by this earthly gravity, if you were to learn to understand the whole organism of the cow as it lies in the meadow digesting, and in this process of digestion manifesting wonderful revelations from the astrality of the universe, you would also learn how to make what can be weighed, measured and counted into a system with which you could overcome all other forms of civilization and impose on the whole globe a civilization which would do nothing but weigh, count and measure, making everything else disappear. For what would result from initiation into the organization of the cow? That is a question of utmost gravity, a question of immense significance. What would be the result?

Well, the way in which people construct machines, for instance, varies greatly according to the nature of the machine in question; at present machines are still imperfect and primitive, but everything tends towards the gradual development of a kind of machine that depends on oscillations, in which oscillation, vibration and sequential motion produce the machine's effect. Everything is tending towards such machines. But if machines can be constructed that function together in the way that can be learned from the distribution of foodstuffs in the organization of the cow, then the oscillations produced by the machines on earth, these small earth-oscillations, will be such that what is above the earth will oscillate in harmony with what is happening on the earth; then the movements of our planetary system would be compelled to oscillate in harmony with the earth's system, just as a string tuned to a certain pitch vibrates in sympathy when another one is struck in the same room.

That is the terrible law of oscillations sounding in unison that would be fulfilled if the alluring call of the cow so seduces the Orient that the East would then be able to wholly penetrate the unspiritual, purely mechanistic civilization of the West and Centre. It would then become possible to create on the earth a mechanistic system engineered to precisely match the mechanistic system of the universe. Everything connected with the activities of the air, of the environment, and everything connected with the activities of the stars, would be exterminated from human civilization. What human beings experience, for instance, through the cycle of the year, what they experience through living together with the sprouting, budding life of spring, with the fading, dying life of autumn— all this would lose its significance for them. Human civilization would resound with the clattering and rattling of oscillating machines and with the echo of this clattering and rattling, which would stream down to earth from the cosmos as a reaction to this mechanization of the earth.

If you observe a part of what is active at the present time, you will say to yourselves: A part of our present-day civilization is actually on the way to having this terrible element of decline and fall as its goal.

Now turn your thoughts to what would happen if the Centre fell prey to the allurements of what is spoken by the lion. It is true that the danger I have just described would then not be present. Mechanization would gradually disappear from the face of the earth. Civilization would not become mechanistic, but, with one-sided power, man would be given over to all that lives in wind and weather, in the cycle of the year. People would be yoked to the year's course, and thereby compelled to live particularly in the interaction of their rhythms of breathing and circulation. They would primarily develop what involuntary life provides, i.e. chest nature.

Through this, however, such human egoism would overcome earth civilization that everyone would be intent on living for himself alone and no one would bother about anything save his own immediate well-being. That is the temptation to which the civilization of the Centre is exposed; such is the existence which could hang like fate over the civilization of the earth.

And yet again, if the alluring call of the eagle were to seduce the West so that it would succeed in spreading its way of thinking and attitude of mind over the whole earth, binding itself up in a one-sided way in this kind of thinking and attitude, then in humanity as a whole there would arise the urge to enter into direct connection with the supersensible world as this once was in the beginning, at the outset of Earth evolution. People would feel the urge to extinguish what man has won for himself in freedom and independence. They would come to live only and entirely in that unconscious will which allows the gods to live in human muscles and nerves. They would revert to primitive clairvoyance. Man would seek to free himself from the earth by turning back to the earth's beginnings.

For exact clairvoyant vision all this is further emphasized through the fact that one continually hears within one what may be called the voice of the grazing cow, which says: 'Do not look upwards; all power comes from the earth. Learn to know all that lies in the earth's activity. You will be the lord of the earth. You will perpetuate the results of your work on earth.' Yes, if man were to succumb to this alluring call, it would be impossible to avoid the danger of which I have spoken: the mechanizing of the earth's civilization. For the astrality of this animal of digestion wants to make the present enduring, to make the present eternal. From the lion organization proceeds not what wants to make the present endure, but rather what would make the present as fleeting as possible, what would make everything a mere sport of the continually repeating cycle of the year, and would spend itself in wind and weather, in the play of the sunbeams, in the currents of the air. And civilization, too, would take on this character.

If, with real understanding, one contemplates the eagle as it soars through the air, it appears as though it were bearing in its plumage the memory of what was there at the very inception of the earth. The eagle has preserved in its plumage the forces that still worked into the earth from above. It can be said that in every eagle we see the past millennia of the earth; with its physical nature the eagle has not touched the earth, or at the most only for the purpose of seizing its prey, and in no way for the satisfaction of its own life. To fulfil its own life, the eagle circles in the air because it is indifferent to what has developed on the earth, because it takes joy and inspiration from the forces of the air, because it actually despises the life of earth and wishes to live in the element in which the earth itself lived when it was not yet earth, but, in the beginning of its evolution, was still imbuing itself with heavenly forces. The eagle is the proud creature that would not partake in the evolution of the solid earth, which withdrew from the influence of this solidifying process and wished to remain united only with the forces which were there at the inception of the earth.

Such are the teachings given to us by this threefold representation of the animal kingdom, if we can conceive it as an immense and mighty script, written into the universe for the elucidation of its riddles. For, in very truth, every single thing in the universe is a written character if we could but read it. And especially when we can read their connection, we understand the riddle of the universe.

How full of significance it is when we realize: What we do when we measure with compasses or measuring rod, when we weigh with the scales, when we count—this is in fact only the assembling of something fragmentary; it becomes a whole when we understand the organization of the cow in its inner spirituality. This is what it means to read the secrets of the universe. And this reading of the universe's secrets leads to understanding the being of the world and of man. This is modern initiation wisdom. It is this which at the present time, needs to be said out of the depths of spiritual life.

It is difficult indeed for human beings to be human today. For, if I may put it so, confronted by the three animal forces man conducts himself like the antelope in the fable which I told you yesterday. What strives to be one-sided takes on a correspondingly altered form. The lion remains lion, but it wishes to have the other animal representatives metamorphosed into fellow beasts of prey. Thus for what in truth is eagle it substitutes a fellow beast of prey, the hyena, whose nature it is to live on what is dead, on that element of death which is produced in our head, and which continually at every moment contributes atomistic particles towards our death. So the fable replaces the eagle with the hyena, the hyena which consumes decay; and in the place of the cow—in line with the decline I have referred to—the lion puts its fellow beast of prey, the wolf. Thus we have another threefold animal group in the fable—the lion, the hyena and the wolf. And when today there are three contrasting, alluring calls, cosmic symbolism, one can say, manifests this contrast: the eagle gradually sinks to earth and becomes the hyena, and the cow no longer desires in its holy, patient way to be an image of the cosmos, but becomes the ravening wolf.

And now we can translate the legend with which I ended my lecture yesterday from the old African version into one of modern civilization. Yesterday I narrated this legend from what may be called the African point of view: The lion, the wolf and the hyena went out hunting. They killed an antelope. First the hyena was asked to divide the prey; it apportioned it according to hyena logic and said: 'A third for everyone: a third for the lion, a third for the wolf, and a third for me.' Whereupon the hyena was consumed. And now the lion said to the wolf, 'You divide it.' So the wolf said, 'You get the first third because you have killed the hyena and therefore the hyena's share is also your due. The second third is yours too because, according to the verdict of the hyena, you would have had a third in any case, for each of us was to have had a third; and you get the last third as well because of all the beasts you are the wisest and bravest.' And the lion said to the wolf, 'Who taught you to divide in so excellent a way?' The wolf said, 'The hyena taught me.'

The logic is the same in both cases, but in its application to reality something quite different results according to whether the hyena applied the logic, or the wolf with the hyena's experience. It is the application of logic to reality that matters.

Now we can also translate this fable into what I may call the version of modern civilization and tell the story somewhat differently. But please note that I am always speaking of what really matters in the whole great process of civilization. Thus, expressed in modern fashion, the story could perhaps run as follows: The antelope is killed. The hyena withdraws and delivers a silent verdict; it does not dare to arouse ill-feeling in the lion. It withdraws, delivers a silent verdict, and waits in the background. The lion and the wolf now begin to fight over the body of the antelope. They fight and fight, until they have so severely wounded each other that both die from their wounds. Now the hyena comes and consumes antelope, wolf and lion, after they have entered into a state of decay. The hyena is the image of what lies in the human intellect, the element in human nature which kills. It is the reverse side, the caricature, of eagle civilization.

If you feel what I wish to convey by the Europeanizing of the old African fable, you will recognize that these things need to be rightly understood at the present time. But they will only be rightly understood when man learns to oppose the three-fold alluring call—the call of the eagle, of the lion, and of the cow—with what he himself should utter, an utterance which

today should be the watchword in all we humans do to gain in
strength, in our thinking, and deeds:

> I must learn
> Your power, O Cow,
> From the language
> Which the stars reveal in me.

We need to learn not only about earth's gravity, not merely
to weigh, measure and count, nor learn merely of what lies in
the physical organization of the cow, but of what is embodied
in it; humbly to turn our gaze away from this organization and
up to the heights. Then what would otherwise become the
mechanistic civilization of the earth will be spiritualized.

And the second utterance of the human being must be:

> I must learn
> Your power, O Lion,
> From the language
> Which, through year and day,
> Surrounding life engenders in me.

Notice the words 'reveal', and 'engenders'.
And the third utterance which man must learn is:

> I must learn
> Your power, O Eagle,
> From the language
> Which earth-sprung life creates in me.

Thus man must oppose his threefold utterance to the one-
sided alluring calls, that threefold utterance whose meaning
can bring what is one-sided into harmonious balance. He
must learn to look towards the cow, but then, after entering
deeply into an inner experience of its nature, turn his gaze
upwards to what is revealed by the language of the stars. He
must learn to direct his gaze upwards to the eagle, but then,
after deeply experiencing within himself the eagle's nature, he

must look down with the clear gaze that the eagle's nature has bestowed on him and behold what springs and sprouts forth from the earth, and what also works from below upwards in the organization of man. And he must learn to so behold the lion that the lion reveals to him what blows around him in the wind, what flashes towards him in the lightning, what rumbles around him in the thunder, what wind and weather in the course of the seasons bring about in the life of the earth into which man himself is yoked. Thus, when man directs his physical gaze upwards and his spiritual gaze downwards, his physical gaze downwards and his spiritual gaze upwards, his physical gaze out towards the east and his spiritual gaze in the opposite direction, towards the west—when in other words man allows above and below, forwards and backwards, spiritual gaze and physical gaze to interpenetrate each other, then he will be able to receive and understand the true calls, bringing him strength and not weakness—the call of the eagle from the heights, that of the lion from the surrounding world, that of the cow from the interior of the earth.

This is what man should learn about his connection with the universe, so that he may become ever more capable of working for earth-civilization, and of serving its ascent instead of its decline.

> Learn to know my nature!
> I give you the power
> To create a universe
> In your own head.

Thus speaks the Eagle.
West

> Learn to know my nature!
> I give you the power
> To embody the universe
> In the radiance of the encircling air.

Thus speaks the Lion.
Centre

Learn to know my nature!
I give you the power
To wrest from the universe
Measure, number and weight.

Thus speaks the Cow.
Orient

I must learn
Your power, O Cow,
From the language
Which the stars reveal in me.

I must learn
Your power, O Lion,
From the language
Which, through year and day,
Surrounding life engenders in me.

I must learn
Your power, O Eagle,
From the language
Which earth-sprung life creates in me.

Lecture 3

21 October 1923

We have tried, again from a particular aspect, to place the human being into the universe. Today we wish to put the subject forward in a way which will weld everything into a whole. During our physical life we live on the earth; we are surrounded by events and facts which are there because of the physical matter of the earth. This matter is moulded and shaped in the most varied manner to create everything that exists in the kingdoms of nature, and also the human form itself. The physical matter of the earth is part of everything that exists on earth. Today—because we shall immediately have to speak about its opposite—let us call this matter the physical substance of the earth, comprising all that provides the material basis for the various earthly forms; and then let us differentiate from it everything in the universe which is the opposite of physical substance, namely, spiritual substance. This last is the basis not only of our own soul, but also of all those configurations in the universe which, as spiritual configurations, are connected with physical configurations.

It is not right to speak only of physical matter or physical substance. Think only of the fact that we needed to place into our total picture of the world the beings of the higher hierarchies. These beings of the higher hierarchies have no earthly substance, no physical substance, in what might be called their 'body'. What they have is spiritual substance. When we look upon what is earthly we become aware of physical substance; when we look upon what is beyond the earthly we become aware of spiritual substance.

Today people know little of spiritual substance. That is why they speak of the earth being who belongs in both the physical and the spiritual world—the human being—as though he too only possessed physical substance. This, however, is not the case. Man bears both spiritual and physical substance in himself in so remarkable a way as to astonish anyone who is not accustomed to pay heed to such matters. If, for example, we consider the element in human beings that leads them into movement, namely, what is connected with the human limb system and its inward continuation, which is metabolic activity, it is incorrect to speak primarily of physical substance. You will soon see this more clearly. We only speak correctly about the human being when we regard the so-called lower part of human nature as having its basis, in fact, in spiritual substance.

So that if we were to represent the human being in a diagram we would have to say: The lower man actually shows us a formation in spiritual substance, and the further towards the human head we go, the more the human being is made of physical substance. The head is essentially made of physical substance. But of the legs—grotesque through this may sound—it must be said that essentially they are made of spiritual substance. So that as we approach the head we must draw the human being in such a way that we allow spiritual substance to change gradually into physical substance; physical substance is to be found particularly in the human head. Spiritual substance, on the other hand, is spread out in a particularly beautiful way just where—if I may put it so—man extends his legs and his arms into space. It is really as though the most important matter for arm and leg is precisely the fact that they are filled with spiritual substance, as if this is their essence. In the case of arm and leg, it is really as though the physical substance were only floating in spiritual substance, whereas the head presents a compact form composed of physical substance. In a form such as man possesses, however, we must differentiate not only the *substance*, but also the *forces*. And here again we must distinguish between spiritual forces and earthly, physical forces.

In the case of these forces, things are exactly the opposite. In the limbs and metabolism the substance is spiritual but the forces are physical, for instance the force of gravity in the legs. In the head the substance is physical but the forces active within it are spiritual. Spiritual forces play through the head; physical forces play through the spiritual substance of the limbs and metabolism. The human being can only be fully understood when we distinguish in him the upper region, his head and also the upper part of the chest, as actual physical substance worked through by spiritual forces, the lowest of which, one can say, are active in the breathing. And we must regard the lower part of man as a formation composed of spiritual substance within which physical forces are working. Only we must be clear as to how these things are interrelated in man, for the human being also projects his head nature into his whole organism so that the head, which is what it is because it is composed of physical substance worked through by spiritual forces, also projects its entire nature into the lower part of the human being; and what man is because of his spiritual substance in which physical forces are at work, this, on the other hand, plays upwards into the upper part of the organism. In these activities in the human being there is mutual interaction. Man can in fact only be understood when he is regarded in this way, as composed of physical and spiritual substantiality and of physical and spiritual dynamic forces.

This is something of great significance. For if we look away from external phenomena and enter into man's inner nature, it becomes clear to us that disturbance and irregularity ought not to enter into this distribution of substance and of forces in the human being.

If, for example, what should be pure substance, pure spiritual substance in man, is too strongly penetrated by physical matter, by physical substance—if, that is to say, physical substance which should in fact tend upwards towards the head makes itself too strongly felt in the metabolism so that head nature enters too powerfully into the metabolism, the human being becomes ill; certain quite definite types of illness then arise. And the task of healing consists in paralyzing and driving out this physical substance formation intruding into spiritual substantiality. On the other hand, if man's metabolic system, with its particular and special manner of being worked through by physical forces in spiritual substance, is sent up towards the head, then the head is, as it were, too strongly spiritualized, and excessive spiritualization of the head results. This also represents a condition of illness, and care must then be taken to send enough physical forces of nutrition to the head, and in a way which does not allow them to become spiritualized.

Anyone who turns his attention to human beings in health and sickness will very soon be able to perceive the usefulness of this differentiation if he is really concerned with truth and not with outer appearance. But something of a very different nature also comes into this. What human beings feel themselves to be, because they are constituted in the way I have described, initially remains below in the subconscious for ordinary consciousness today. It does exist there, certainly, as a kind of mood, a kind of life-mood. But it is spiritual vision alone that brings it to full consciousness, and I can only describe this spiritual vision to you as follows. Anyone who, through modern initiation science, knows this secret of the human being—that it is actually the head which is the main, the most essential organ needing physical substance, that it is head in order that it may work spiritual forces into that substance; anyone who also knows that the most essential thing in the system of limbs and metabolism is spiritual substance and that this needs physical forces—the forces of gravity, of balance and the other physical forces—in order to exist; anyone who can thus penetrate this secret of the human being with spiritual vision and who then turns his gaze back to human, earthly existence—must acknowledge his tremendous debt to the world. For he must admit that in order to maintain his human existence he requires certain conditions; and that through these very conditions he owes a debt to the earth. He is continuously withdrawing something from the earth. And he finds himself obliged to say that the spiritual substance which he bears within himself as man during earthly existence is actually needed by the earth. When man passes through death, he should in fact leave this spiritual substance behind him for the earth, for the earth continually needs spiritual substance for its renewal. But this man cannot do, for he would then be unable to undertake the path he travels, as human being, through the period after death. He must take this spiritual substance with him for the life between death and a new birth; he needs it, for he would disappear, so to speak, after death if he did not take this spiritual substance with him.

Only by taking the spiritual substance of his limbs and metabolism through the gate of death can man undergo the transformations he needs to undergo. He would be unable to descend to future incarnations if he were to give back to the earth the spiritual substance which he owes to it. This he cannot do. He remains a debtor. And that is something which there is no means of bettering as long as the earth remains in its middle period. At the end of earth existence things will be otherwise.

It is indeed the case, my dear friends, that one who beholds life with spiritual vision has not only the sufferings and sorrows—perhaps also the happiness and joy—that are offered by ordinary life. The beholding of the spiritual brings cosmic feelings, cosmic sufferings and joys. And initiation is inseparable from the appearance of such cosmic suffering. For example, one has to admit that simply by maintaining our humanity we have to become debtors to the earth. I cannot give to the earth what I really should give if, in a cosmic sense, I were to act with complete rectitude.

Matters are similar as regards the substance which is present in the head. Because throughout the entire course of earthly life spiritual forces are working in the physical substance of the head, this head substance becomes estranged from the earth. Man must remove from the earth the substance for his head. But in order to be man, he must also continually imbue this substance of his head with extraterrestrial spiritual forces. And when the human being dies, this is something extremely disturbing to the earth, because it must now take back the substance of the human head which has become so foreign to it. When the human being has gone through the gate of death and yields up his head substance to the earth, then this head substance—which is now spiritualized and bears within itself what results from the spiritual—does in fact act as a poison, as a really disturbing element in the totality of the life of the earth. When man sees into the truth of these matters he is obliged to say to himself that the honest thing would be to take this substance with him through the gate of death, for it would in fact be much better suited to the spiritual region which man traverses between death and a new birth. He cannot do this. For if man were to take this spiritualized earth substance with him, he would continually create something adverse to all his development between death and a new birth. It would be the most terrible thing that could happen to man if he were to take this spiritualized head substance with him. It would work incessantly on the negation of his spiritual development between death and rebirth.

One must therefore acknowledge when one sees into the truth of these things, that here too man becomes a debtor to the earth; for something for which he is indebted to the earth but has made useless for it, this he must continually leave behind, he cannot take it with him. What man should leave for the earth he takes from it; what man should take with him, what he has made useless for the earth, this he gives over to it with his earthly dust, thus causing the earth immense suffering in the totality of its life, the wholeness of its being.

Spiritual vision, it is true, at first leaves a heavy weight on the human soul, something like a tremendous feeling of tragedy. And only when one surveys wider epochs of time, when one beholds the evolution of entire systems, only then is the prospect revealed that in later stages of human evolution, when the earth eventually approaches its end—in the Jupiter, Venus and Vulcan stages—man will be able to restore the balance, to annul the debt.

Thus it is not only by going through the experiences of a single life that man fashions karma, but man creates karma—world karma, cosmic karma—just through the fact that he is an earthly human being, an inhabitant of the earth; and draws his substance from the earth.

It is then possible to look away from man, to look towards the rest of the natural world and see how—though man must burden himself with the debt of which I have just told you—balance is nevertheless continually restored by cosmic beings. And here one penetrates into wonderful secrets of existence, into secrets which must be seen in conjunction with each other before they become something from which one can gain a conception of the wisdom of the world.

Let us turn our gaze away from man and towards something which has claimed much of our attention during the last few days; let us turn our gaze to the world of the birds, represented for us by the eagle. We spoke of the eagle as the representative of the bird world, as the creature which had all the characteristics and forces of the bird kingdom. When we consider the eagle, we are in fact considering the function of the bird world as a whole within the great cosmic scheme of things. In future, therefore, I shall simply speak of 'the eagle'.

I have told you how the eagle actually corresponds to the head of man, and how the forces which give rise to thoughts in the human head give rise to the eagle's plumage. So that the sun-irradiated, light-imbued forces of the air are actually working in the plumage. This is what shimmers in the eagle's plumage—the light-irradiated power of the air.

Now the eagle—to which many bad qualities may certainly be ascribed—does nevertheless possess, as regards its cosmic existence, the remarkable attribute that every part of it that is created by the sun-irradiated forces of the air remains outside the skin, in the configuration of the plumage. What takes place here is, in fact, only to be noticed when the eagle dies.

For it is only when the eagle dies that one becomes aware of what a remarkably superficial digestion it has compared to the thorough-going digestion of the cow with its process of chewing the cud. The cow is really the animal of digestion— again as representative of many creatures of the animal kingdom. Here digestion is thoroughly performed. The eagle, like all birds, digests in a superficial way, only begins the business of digestion. Digestion plays only a small part in the eagle's whole existence, is merely a subsidiary process and is treated as such. On the other hand, everything in the eagle which has to do with plumage is formed with enormous care. In the case of some other birds this is even more so. Such a feather is indeed a wonderful structure. Here we find most strongly in evidence what may be called earthly matter, which the eagle has taken from the earth; this is spiritualized by the forces of the heights but in such a way that the eagle does not make it its own, for the eagle makes no claim to reincarnation. It need not, therefore, be troubled about what is being brought about in the earthly matter of its plumage through the spiritual forces of the heights; it need not be troubled about how this works on in the spiritual world.

Now, when the eagle dies and its feathers fall into decay—as already mentioned this is also true for all other birds—the spiritualized earthly matter goes out into spirit land and is changed back into spiritual substance.

You see the relationship between our head and the eagle is a strange one. What we cannot do, the eagle can; it can remove from the earth what has been spiritualized in the earth through spiritual forces working on earthly substance.

This, too, is why we have such a strange feeling when we observe an eagle in flight. We feel it to be something foreign to the earth, something which has more to do with the heavens than with the earth, although it draws its physical substance from the earth. But how does it do this? It obtains its substance by stealing it from the earth, it is just a robber. One might say that according to what may be called the ordinary, commonplace law of earth existence no provision was made for the eagle to get anything. It becomes a robber and steals physical matter, as is done in all sorts of ways by the bird kingdom as a whole. But the eagle does restore the balance. It steals the physical matter it needs but then allows it to be spiritualized by the forces which exist as spiritual forces in the upper regions; and after death it carries off into spirit land the spiritualized earth forces which it had stolen. With the eagle spiritualized earth matter goes out into spirit land.

Now the life of animals also does not come to an ultimate end when they die. They have their significance in the universe. A physical eagle in flight is only a symbol of its real being, as it were. That is how it flies as a physical eagle. Oh, but it flies on after death! The spiritualized physical matter of the eagle's nature flies into the far distance in order to unite itself with the spiritual substance of spirit land.

You see what wonderful secrets of the universe one comes upon when one enters into the reality of these things. Only then does one really learn why the various animal and other forms exist on earth. They all have their great and immense significance in the whole universe.

And now let us go to the other extreme, to something which we have also studied during these days; let us turn to the cow, so venerated by the Hindus. There we have the opposite extreme. Just as the eagle is very similar to the human head, so is the cow very similar to the human metabolic system. The cow is the animal of digestion. And strange as it sounds, this animal of digestion consists essentially of spiritual substance into which the physical matter consumed is merely integrated and diffused. There in the cow you have the spiritual substance [*drawing on the board*] and physical substance penetrates here everywhere and is absorbed, digested by the spiritual substance. It is in order that this may happen in a really thorough way that the process of digestion is so thorough and comprehensive in the cow. It is really the most thorough digestive process that can be conceived, and in this respect—if I may put it so— the cow is really most thorough in the business of being an animal. It is thoroughly animal and actually brings animal nature—this animal egoism, this animal egoity—down to earth from the universe and into the sphere of earth's gravity.

No other animal has the same relation between blood-weight and total body-weight as the cow; other animals have either less or more blood than the cow in proportion to the weight of the body. Weight has to do with gravity and the blood with individual existence; not with the ego, for this is only possessed by man, but with separate, individual existence. The blood also makes the animal an animal—the higher animal at least. And we might say that the cow has solved the universal problem of the right relation between the weight of the blood and the weight of the whole body—if one wishes to be as thoroughly animal as possible.

You see, it was not for nothing that the ancients called the zodiac 'the circle of animal figures'.* The zodiac is twelvefold; its totality is divided into twelve separate parts. The forces which emerge from the zodiac in the cosmos take on form and shape in the animals. But the other animals do not conform to the zodiacal proportion so exactly. The cow has a twelfth part of her body weight in the weight of her blood. Her blood weight is a twelfth part of her body weight. In the donkey it is only a twenty-third part and in the dog a tenth part. All the other animals have a different proportion. In the case of man the blood is one thirteenth of the body weight.

You see, the cow aims to express the whole of animal nature in terms of weight, to bring something cosmic to expression in the most thorough way possible. A fact I have mentioned repeatedly during these days, namely, that the astral body of the cow shows that it actually brings a higher principle to realization in physical matter—this comes to expression in the fact that the cow maintains the division into twelve in her own inner ratio of weights. There you have the cosmic principle in the cow. Everything to do with the cow is of such a nature that the forces of the earth are worked into spiritual substance. In the cow, earth heaviness is obliged to distribute itself according to zodiacal proportion. Earth heaviness must allow a twelfth part of itself to be subsumed in individual existence. Everything that the cow possesses by way of spiritual substance forces it to enter into earthly conditions.

Thus the cow lying in the meadow is in actual fact spiritual substance that takes up earthly matter, absorbs it and makes it similar to itself.

When the cow dies the spiritual substance which it bears within it can be taken up by the earth, together with its earthly matter, to benefit the life of the whole earth. And man is right to regard the cow as the true beast of sacrifice, for essentially she continually gives to the earth what it needs, without which

* In German, 'Tierkreis'—circle of animals.

it could not continue to exist and would harden and dry up. She continually gives spiritual substance to the earth and renews the earth's inner mobility, its inner living quality.

When you behold on the one hand a meadow with its cattle, and on the other hand the eagle in flight, then you have a remarkable contrast: the eagle which, when it dies, takes away into the expanses of spirit land the earth matter that has become spiritualized and therefore useless for the earth; and the cow which, when it dies, gives heavenly matter to the earth for its renewal. The eagle takes from the earth what the earth can no longer use, what must return to spirit land. The cow carries into the earth what the earth continually needs as forces of renewal from spirit land.

Here you see something like an upsurge of feelings and perceptions arising from initiation science. People usually believe that one can certainly study this initiation science, but that it results in nothing but concepts and ideas. One fills one's head with ideas about the non-physical world, just as one otherwise fills one's head with ideas about the things of the physical world. But this is not how it is. Penetrating ever further into this initiation science, we reach the point of drawing forth from the depths of the soul feelings and perceptions the existence of which we formerly did not even surmise, but which nevertheless are there unconsciously in every human being; we reach the point of experiencing all existence differently from the way we experienced it before. And so I can describe to you an experience which actually belongs to the living comprehension of spiritual science, of initiation science. It is the experience of having to say to ourselves that if man alone were on earth, we would—if we recognized his true nature—have to despair of the earth ever receiving what it needed: spiritualized matter withdrawn and spirit substance bestowed at the right time. We should really have to experience the contrast between human existence and the earth's existence, a feeling that causes great, great pain, for we have to admit that if man is to be rightly man on the earth, the earth cannot be rightly earth because of man. Man and earth have need of each other, but man and earth cannot mutually support each other. What the one needs is lost to the other; what the other needs is lost to the first. And we should have no security as regards the life-relationship between man and earth were it not that the surrounding world enables us to say: What the human being is unable to achieve in taking spiritualized earth substance over into spirit land is accomplished by the bird kingdom; and what man is unable to do in giving spiritual substance to the earth is accomplished by the animals which chew the cud, as represented by the cow.

In this way the world is rounded into a whole. If we look only at man, uncertainty enters our feelings as regards existence on the earth; if we look at what surrounds man, our feeling of certainty is restored.

And now you will wonder even less that a religious world conception, which penetrates so deeply into the spiritual as does Hinduism, venerates the cow, for it is the animal which continually spiritualizes the earth and continually gives to the earth that spiritual substance which it has taken from the cosmos. And we really should allow the following image to become real in our minds: beneath a grazing herd of cattle, the earth is quickened to joyful vigorous life, and the elemental spirits down there rejoice because they are assured of their nourishment from the cosmos through the existence of the creatures grazing above them. And we ought to paint a picture of the dancing, rejoicing airy sphere of the elemental spirits hovering around the eagle. Then we would portray spiritual realities, and the physical would be seen within spiritual realities; we would see the eagle extending outwards in his aura, and the rejoicing of the elemental air spirits and fire spirits of the air playing into that aura.

We would see that remarkable aura of the cow which is in such marked contrast to earthly existence because it is entirely cosmic; we would see lively merriment in the senses of the elemental earth spirits, who are here able to perceive what they have lost by being constrained to live out their existence in the darkness of the earth. For these spirits what appears in the cow is sun. The elemental spirits whose dwelling place is in the earth cannot rejoice in the physical sun, but they can rejoice in the astral bodies of the animals which chew the cud.

Yes, my dear friends, there does indeed exist a natural history which is different from that found today in books. What is actually the end result of the natural history found today in books?

The sequel to the book by Albert Schweitzer, which I discussed some time ago, has just appeared. You may remember my review of this small volume on the state of modern civilization, which appeared some time back in *The Goetheanum*.* The preface to this sequel is in fact representative of a somewhat sorry chapter of modern thought. In the first small volume, which I also reviewed, there was at least a certain force of argument and the insight to admit what our civilization lacks. The preface to this second volume is a really sorry chapter. For Schweitzer here takes credit to himself for being the first to perceive that, fundamentally, knowledge alone can provide absolutely nothing, and that ethics and a world conception must be gained from somewhere other than knowledge.

Now in the first place much has been said about the limits of knowledge, and it is—how shall I put it—a trifle short-sighted to believe that one has been the first to speak about the limits of knowledge. This has been done by natural scientists in every possible way. So there is no need to pride oneself on being the first to discover this colossal error.

---

* First published, in German, in *Das Goetheanum*, No. 47, 1 July 1923; now in *Der Goetheanumgedanke inmitten der Kulturkrisis der Gegenwart* (GA 36). Not available in English.

Apart from this, however, it emerges that such an excellent thinker as Schweitzer—for he is an excellent thinker, as his first small volume certainly shows—has reached the conclusion that if we wish to have a world conception, if we wish to have ethics, then we must entirely do without science and knowledge, for these in fact give us nothing. Recognized science and knowledge, as put forward today in books, do not enable us—as Schweitzer says—to discover meaning in the universe. Essentially, if one looks at the world the way these individuals do one cannot avoid the conclusion that eagles in their flight have no purpose apart from the fact that they can be used in making armorial crests; cows are useful here on earth because they give milk, and so on. But because man also is regarded only as a physical being, he only has physical usefulness; and all this has no meaning for the world as a whole.

If people are unwilling to go further than this they will certainly not reach the level where the world can be seen to have meaning. We must pass on to what the spiritual, to what initiation science can say to us about the world; then we shall certainly discover the meaning of the world. Then we shall find this meaning of the world as we discover wonderful mysteries in all existence—mysteries such as that which unfolds in connection with the dying eagle and the dying cow; and between them the dying lion which in its turn holds spiritual substance and physical substance in balance within itself through the harmony it establishes in the rhythm of breathing and of blood. We shall find that it is the lion whose group soul regulates how many eagles and how many cows are necessary to enable the correct process to take its course in the upward and also in the downward direction, in the way I have described to you.

You see, the three animals, eagle, lion and ox or cow, were created out of a wonderful instinctive knowledge. Their connection with man is one we can sense and feel. For when he sees into the truth of these things, the human being should really admit: The eagle relieves me of the tasks that I myself cannot fulfil through my head; the cow relieves me of the tasks that I myself cannot fulfil through my metabolism and through my limbs; the lion relieves me of the tasks that I myself cannot fulfil through my rhythmical system. And thus I myself and the three animals are made into a whole in the great cosmic scheme of things.

Thus one lives one's way into cosmic relationships. Thus one feels the deep connections in the world and learns to know how wise are the powers which hold sway in the living world into which man is woven and which billow and surge around him.

You see, in this way we were able to interweave everything that we encountered when we sought to discover man's connection with the three animal forces which we have spoken about in recent weeks.

Part Two

The Inner Connection of World Phenomena and the Essential Nature of the World

'Cosmic activity is indeed the greatest of artists. The cosmos fashions everything according to laws which bring the deepest satisfaction to the artistic sense.'

Lecture 4

26 October 1923

We have studied certain aspects of the connection between earth* conditions, cosmic conditions, animals and man and shall continue with these studies during the coming days. Today, however, I wish to find the transition to still broader spheres that we shall have to consider in future. I should like, in the first place, to draw attention to what has already been described in my *Occult Science* as the evolution of the earth in the cosmos—beginning with the primordial Saturn metamorphosis of the earth. This Saturn condition must be thought of as already containing within itself everything belonging to our planetary system. The separate planets of our planetary system, from Saturn onwards to the moon, were at that time still within old Saturn—which, as you know, consisted only of heat ether—as undifferentiated world bodies. Saturn, which had not even attained to the density of air but was merely heat ether, contained in an undifferentiated etheric condition everything which later became independent and took individual form in the separate planets.

We then distinguish as the second metamorphosis of Earth evolution what, in a comprehensive sense, I have called the old Sun metamorphosis of the earth. Here we have to do with

---

* In what follows, the planetary stages of earth's evolution will be designated with initial capitals (e.g. 'Moon'), whereas the planetary bodies as they are today are in lower case ('the moon'). The distinction between these two, however, is not always clear.—Ed.

the gradual evolution from the fire globe of Saturn to the air globe, the light-permeated, light-irradiated, glittering air globe of the sun.

Then we have a third metamorphosis out of which, after the earlier conditions had been recapitulated, there evolved on the one hand all that was of a sun nature which at that time still comprised the earth and moon—all this is described in *Occult Science*—and all that was already externalized and to which Saturn in its state of separation belonged.

At the same time, however, during this period of the Moon metamorphosis, we meet the fact that the sun separated from what was now a blend of earth and moon. I have often described how the kingdoms of nature which we know today did not then exist and how the earth did not enclose a mineral mass, but was, if I may so express myself, of the nature of horn, so that the solid constituents freed themselves, forming rock-like projections of horny substance, jutting out from the moon mass which was now the consistency of water. Then there arose the conditions of the fourth metamorphosis, which are the earth conditions of today.

Now if we draw a diagram of these four metamorphoses in their sequence we have first the Saturn condition as a body of heat (drawing on the blackboard) that still contained dissolved within it everything later contained in our planetary system; then we draw the Sun metamorphosis, the Moon metamorphosis and the Earth metamorphosis. Two things can be distinguished within these four stages.

Just consider how during the evolution of Saturn and on into the Sun epoch substance had only advanced to a gaseous state! Evolution took its start from the globe of fire; the fiery globe was then metamorphosed and densified into a globe of air, which however was already imbued and glittering with light. Here we have the first part of evolution.

Then we have the part of evolution in which the Moon first plays a role. For it is the role played by Moon evolution which enabled it to fashion those horny rock formations. And during the Earth metamorphosis the moon separated off and became a satellite, leaving the inner earth forces behind for the Earth stage. The forces of gravity, for instance, are definitely forces that have remained behind from Moon evolution as something physical. The earth would never have developed the forces of gravity had not residues remained from when the old Moon was part of it. The moon itself departed; it is that colony in cosmic space about which I spoke to you from its spiritual aspect only a few days ago. Its substantiality is quite different from that of the earth, but it left behind in the earth what, speaking in a wider sense, may be called the earth's magnetism. The forces of the earth, namely, the forces of gravity and the effects defined as the effects of weight, have remained over from Moon evolution. And thus we can say that on the one hand we have here (see diagram page 66) in the Saturn and Sun condition the essentially warm, light-irradiated metamorphosis, if the two are taken together, and on the other hand we have in the Moon and Earth condition the Moon-sustained, watery metamorphosis, a watery condition which evolved during the Moon metamorphosis, and which then remained during the Earth metamorphosis; the solid element is actually called forth by the forces of gravity.

These two pairs of metamorphoses differ from each other to a marked degree, and we must be clear about the fact that everything present in an earlier condition is again inherent in the later one. What constituted the ancient fire globe of Saturn remained as heat substance in all the subsequent metamorphoses; and when today we move about the regions of the earth and everywhere encounter warmth, this warmth is the remains of the ancient Saturn condition. Wherever we find air, or gaseous bodies, we have the remains of ancient Sun evolution. When we look out into the sun-irradiated atmosphere, and have imbued ourselves with feeling and understanding for this Sun epoch of evolution, we can say to ourselves with truth: In this sun-irradiated atmosphere we have remains of the ancient Sun evolution; for had this ancient Sun evolution not taken place, the relationship of our air with the rays of the sun, which are now there outside, would not have existed. Only through the fact that the sun was once united with the earth, that the light of the sun itself shone in the earth—which was still in a gaseous condition, so that the earth was an air globe radiating light into cosmic space— only through this could the later metamorphosis occur, the present Earth metamorphosis, in which the earth is enveloped by an atmosphere of air into which the sun's rays fall from outside. But the sun's rays have a deep inner connection with the earth's atmosphere. They do not, however, impinge—as present-day physicists somewhat crudely state—like small shot projected through the gaseous atmosphere; but the rays of the sun have a deep inner relationship with the air. And this relationship is actually the after-effect of their one-time union during the Sun metamorphosis. Thus everything is mutually interrelated through the fact that the earlier conditions ever and again play into the later conditions in manifold ways. But during the time in which, speaking generally, earth's stages of evolution took their course—as you find in *Occult Science* and as I have briefly sketched it for you here—everything evolved that is on the earth and around it, and also everything that is in the earth.

And now we can say: When we contemplate the present-day earth, we have within it the inner Moon, which produces the solid element, and this is essentially anchored in the earth's magnetism. It is due to the inner Moon that solid matter exists and has weight. It is after all the forces of weight that make fluid into solid. We have next the actual conditions of Earth in the watery element which appears in manifold ways—as ground water for instance, but also in the water which is present in rising vapours, in the rain that comes down, and so on. And further we have in the surrounding atmosphere what is of the nature of air. Moreover all this is permeated by the element of fire, the remains of old Saturn. Even in our present-day earth we are able to point to things that in the realms above us are Sun-Saturn or Saturn-Sun. We can always say to ourselves: Everything which is present in the warm air, which is irradiated with light, is Saturn-Sun. We look up and actually find our air imbued with the effect of Saturn, with the effect of Sun, which in the course of time has evolved into the actual atmosphere of the earth, though this in itself is only an after-effect of the Sun metamorphosis. Broadly speaking, this is what we find when we direct our gaze upwards.

When we direct our gaze downwards, it is more a question of what arose from the last two metamorphoses. We have the heavy, solid element, or better expressed, the working of the forces of weight, the process of solidification; we have the fluid element, we have the Moon-Earth. These two parts of earth existence can be strictly differentiated from each other.

If you read *Occult Science* again with this in mind, you will see that the whole style is such that a marked hiatus occurs at the place where the Sun metamorphosis passes over into the Moon metamorphosis. Even today there is still a kind of sharp contrast between what is above and of the nature of Saturn and what is below and of the nature of the Earth-Moon watery condition.

Thus we can quite well differentiate between the Saturn-Sun gaseous element and the Moon-Earth fluidic element. The one is above, the other below.

When someone who sees into these things with initiation science contemplates the general course of the earth's evolution and everything which has developed along with the earth and belongs to it, his gaze falls first on the manifold variety of the insect world. One can well imagine that the very feeling engendered by the fluttering, glittering insect world would bring us into a certain connection with what is above and of the nature of the Saturn-Sun gaseous condition. And this is indeed the case. When we look at the butterfly with its shimmering colours, we see it fluttering in the air, in the light-flooded, light-irradiated air. It is borne on the waves of the air and barely comes in contact with anything of an Earth-Moon fluid nature. Its element is in the upper regions. And when one investigates the development of this creature, it is a remarkable thing that just in the case of this small insect one arrives at very early epochs of earth metamorphosis. What today shimmers in the light-irradiated air as the butterfly's wings was first formed in germ during old Saturn and developed further during the time of old Sun. It was then that there arose what still today makes it possible for the butterfly to be essentially a creature of light and air. It is thanks to the Sun itself that it can spread light everywhere. But it owes its ability to call forth what is fiery and shimmering in physical substance to the influence of Saturn, Jupiter and Mars. The butterfly's nature cannot be understood if we look for it on the earth.

The forces active in the nature of the butterfly must be sought above, in Sun, Mars, Jupiter, Saturn. And when we go more into the detail of this wonderful development of the butterfly—I have already described it in connection with the human being as what may be called the cosmic embodiment of memory—when we go more into detail, we find in the first place the fluttering butterfly shimmering with light, borne above the earth on the air. It then deposits its egg. Yes, the crude materialist says: 'The butterfly deposits its egg,' because, under the influence of present-day unscientific science, the things of greatest importance are simply not studied. The question is this: To what does the butterfly entrust its egg when it deposits it?

Now investigate any place where the butterfly deposits its egg and everywhere you will find that the egg is deposited in such a way that it cannot be withdrawn from the influence of the sun. The sun's influence on the earth is in fact not only present when the sun is shining directly on to the earth. I have often drawn attention to the fact that in winter farmers put their potatoes into the earth and cover them with it because the sun's warmth and the power of the sunlight that come towards the earth in summer are actually in the earth in winter. On the surface of the earth potatoes become frosted; they do not become frosted but remain really good potatoes if they are buried in a pit and covered with a layer of earth, because throughout the winter the activity of the sun is inside the earth. Throughout the whole winter we must look for the sun activity of summer under the earth. In December, for example, at a certain depth within the earth, we have the July activity of the sun. In July the sun radiates its light and warmth on to the earth's surface. The warmth and light gradually penetrate deeper. And if in December we wish to look for what we experience on the surface of the earth in July, we must dig a pit and then what was on the surface of the earth in July will be found in December at a certain depth within it. There the potato is buried in the July sun. Thus the sun is not only where crude materialistic understanding looks for it; the sun is actually present in many spheres. Only this is strictly regulated according to the seasons of the year in the cosmos.

The butterfly never deposits its eggs where they cannot remain in some way or other in connection with the sun. Consequently one expresses oneself badly when one says that the butterfly lays its eggs in the sphere of the earth. This it does not do at all. It lays its eggs in the sphere of the sun. The butterfly never descends as far down as the earth. Wherever the sun is present in what is earthly, there the butterfly seeks out the place to deposit its eggs so that they remain entirely under the influence of the sun. In no way do they come under the influence of the earth.

Then, as you know, a caterpillar emerges from this butterfly's egg. It remains under the influence of the sun but now comes under another influence as well. The caterpillar would be unable to crawl did it not also come under another influence. And this is the influence of Mars.

If you picture the earth with Mars circling around it, the Mars currents are everywhere in the upper region and also remain there. It is not a question of Mars itself being anywhere in particular, but we have the whole Mars sphere, and the caterpillar as it crawls along does so in the sense of the Mars sphere. Then the caterpillar becomes a chrysalis and builds a cocoon around itself. I described to you how the caterpillar is given up to the sun in this, and the threads are spun in the direction of the line of light. The caterpillar is exposed to the light, follows the rays of light, spins, stops when it is dark, and then goes on spinning. The whole cocoon is actually cosmic sunlight, sunlight which is interwoven with matter. Thus when you have the cocoon of a silkworm, for example—which is used to make your silk garments—what is present in the silk is actually sunlight, into which is spun the substance of the silkworm. Out of its own body the silkworm spins its matter in the direction of the sun's rays, and in this way creates the cocoon around itself. But that this may happen it needs the intervention of Jupiter activity. The sun's rays have to be modified through Jupiter activity.

Then, as you know, the butterfly emerges from the cocoon, from the chrysalis—the butterfly which is borne on the light, and radiant with light. It leaves the dark chamber into which the light could only enter as it did into the cromlechs, in the way I described to you in the case of the ancient Druids' cromlechs. There the sun comes under the influence of Saturn, and it is only in conjunction with Saturn that it can send its light into the air in such a way that the butterfly can shine in the radiance of its many and varied colours.

And thus when we behold that wonderful sea of fluttering butterflies in the atmosphere we must say: That is in truth no earthly creation, but is born into the earth sphere from above.

The butterfly descends no deeper with its egg than to where influences still reach the earth from the sun. The cosmos bestows on the earth the sea of butterflies, Saturn bestows their colours. The sun bestows the power of flight, called forth by the sustaining power of the light, and so on.

Thus I might say that we actually have to see in the butterflies little creatures, strewn down, as it were, on the earth by the sun and what is above the sun in our planetary system. The butterflies, the dragonflies, and the insects in general are actually the gift of Saturn, Jupiter, Mars and the sun. And not a single insect could be produced by the earth, not so much as a flea were it not that the planets beyond the sun together with the sun bestow on the earth the gift of insect life. And we do in truth owe the fact that Saturn, Jupiter, etc. are able to be so generous and allow the insect world to flutter in upon us to the first two stages of metamorphosis which the earth has passed through in its evolution.

And now let us look at the way in which the two last metamorphoses—the Moon condition and the Earth condition—have played their part. In view of the fact that the butterfly's egg is never actually entrusted to the earth, it must be pointed out that at the time when the Moon metamorphosis, the third condition, was beginning, the butterflies were not yet as they are today. The earth too was not so dependent on the sun. At the beginning of the third metamorphosis the sun was actually still united with the earth and only later became separated. The butterfly, therefore, was not so averse to entrusting its embryo to the earth because when it entrusted it to the earth, it was at the same time entrusting it to the sun. Thus here there arose a differentiation. In the case of the first two metamorphoses one can only speak of the early ancestors of the insect world. But at that time to entrust something to the cosmos, to the outer planets and the sun, still meant to entrust it to the earth. Only when the earth condensed, when it acquired water and the mag-

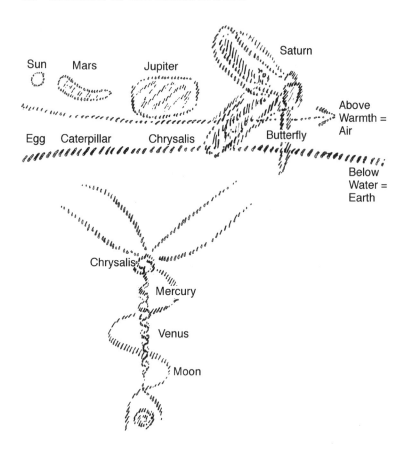

netic forces of the moon, did matters change and a differentiation appear.

Let us assume all this belongs to the upper sphere of warmth and air. Let us now take the lower sphere of water and earth. And let us consider the embryos whose destiny it was to be entrusted to the earth, whereas others were held back and not entrusted to the earth but only to the sun within the earthly.

Now let us consider the embryos which were entrusted to the earth at the time when the third metamorphosis, the

Moon condition, arose. These now came under the influence
of the earth's activity—of the watery earth and moon activity—just as the insect embryos had formerly come under the
influence of the sun activity and of what is beyond the sun.
And through the fact that these embryos came under the
influence of earth-water activity, they became 'plant
embryos'. And the embryos which remained behind in the
upper regions remained insect embryos. When the third
metamorphosis began—through what at the time was of a sun
nature being transformed into what was of the nature of
moon-earth—the plant embryos came into being. And what
you now have in the butterfly under the influence of the extra-
terrestrial cosmos, this whole development from embryo to
caterpillar, from chrysalis to butterfly—this you can now find
in the plant. When the seed became earthly, it was not the
butterfly which developed; but when the seed became earthly
and was entrusted to the earth—not now to the sun—the
plant root developed, the first thing to arise out of the embryo.
And instead of the caterpillar emerging from the chrysalis
under the influence of the forces which proceed from Mars,
the leaf arises, emerging in a rising spiral. The leaf is the
caterpillar which has come under the influence of what is
earthly. When you see the creeping caterpillar you have, in
upper regions, what corresponds below to the leaf of the plant;
this develops out of what became root through the fact that
the seed was transferred from the region of the sun to the
region of the earth.

Proceeding further upwards, you get increasing contraction
until at the top, in the calyx, you have the chrysalis. And
finally the butterfly develops in the flower which is coloured
just like the butterfly in the air. The circle is completed. Just as
the butterfly lays its egg, so does the flower develop within
itself the new seed for the future. So you see, we look up
towards the butterfly and understand it to be the plant raised
up into the air. Under the influence of the sun with the upper

planets the butterfly, from egg to fully developed adult, is the same as the plant is here below under the influence of the earth. When the plant comes into leaf (see diagram) we have from the earth aspect the influence of the moon, then the Venus influence and the Mercury influence. Then there is a return to earth influence. The seed is again under the earth's influence.

We can therefore contemplate two verses which give expression to a great secret of nature:

Behold the plant:
It is the butterfly
Fettered by the earth.
Behold the butterfly:
It is the plant
Freed by the cosmos.

The plant—the butterfly fettered by the earth! The butterfly—the plant freed from the earth by the cosmos!

If one looks at a butterfly, or indeed any insect, from the stage of the egg to when it is fluttering away, it is the plant raised up into the air, fashioned in the air by the cosmos. If one looks at a plant, it is the butterfly held in fetters below. The egg is claimed by the earth. The caterpillar is metamorphosed into leaf formation. The chrysalis formation is metamorphosed into what is contracted in the plant. And then the same principle that unfolds to produce the butterfly develops into the flower in the plant. Small wonder that such an intimate relationship exists between the world of the butterflies, the insect-world in general, and the world of the plants. For in truth the spiritual beings which underlie the insects, the butterflies, must say to themselves: Down here are our relatives; we must maintain allegiance with them, unite ourselves with them—unite ourselves with them in the enjoyment of their juices, and so on, for they are our brothers. They are our brothers who have been metamorphosed down into the domain of the earth, who have become fettered to the earthly, who have won another existence.

And in their turn the spirits who ensoul the plants can look up to the butterflies and say: These are the heavenly relatives of the plant on earth.

You see, one must really say that understanding of the world cannot come about though abstractions, for abstractions do not attain to understanding. Cosmic activity is indeed the greatest of artists. The cosmos fashions everything according to laws which bring the deepest satisfaction to the artistic sense. And no one can understand the butterfly which has sunk down into the earth, unless he metamorphoses abstract thoughts in an artistic sense. No one can understand how that which is contained in the flower of a plant has been raised up into the air by the light and by cosmic forces to be the butterfly, unless once again he can bring abstract thoughts into artistic movement. Nevertheless there always remains something immensely uplifting when we turn our minds to the deep inward connection between the things and beings of nature.

It is a unique experience to see an insect poised on a plant and at the same time to see how astrality holds sway above the blossom. Here the plant is striving away from the earthly. The plant's longing for the heavenly holds sway above the irides-cent petals of the flower. The plant cannot of itself satisfy this longing. Thus there radiates towards it from the cosmos what is of the nature of the butterfly. In beholding this the plant realizes the satisfaction of its own desires. And this is the wonderful relationship existing in the environment of the earth, namely, that the longings of the plant world are assuaged in looking up to the insects, in particular the world of the butterflies. What the blossoming flower longs for, as it radiates its colour out into world space, becomes for it something like known fulfilment when the butterfly approaches it with its shimmer of colours. Longing that makes warmth radiate outwards, satisfaction streaming in from the heavens—this is the interplay between the world of the flowering plants and the world of the butterflies. This is what we should see in the environment of the earth.

Having thus made the transition to the plant world, I shall now be able in the next few days to extend still further the studies which have so far taken us from the human being to the animals. We can now include the plant world, and thus we shall gradually come to man's connection with the whole earth. But for this it was first necessary to build, as it were, a bridge from the fluttering plant of the air, the butterfly, to the butterfly firmly rooted in the earth, the plant. The earthly plant is the firmly rooted butterfly. The butterfly is the flying plant. Having recognized this connection between earth-bound plant and heaven-freed butterfly, we have now established the bridge between animal world and plant world, and thus we can be quite unconcerned by all the inconsequential statements that claim spontaneous generation and the like took place. These prosaic concepts will never lead us into the regions of the universe to which we must attain. Those spheres are only reached when prosaic concepts can be transformed into artistic concepts, so that we may then arrive at an idea of how, from the heaven-born butterfly's egg that was entrusted to the sun alone, the plant later arose: when the butterfly's egg metamorphosed due to the fact that it was no longer entrusted only to the sun, but now developed a connection with the earth.

Lecture 5

27 October 1923

These lectures deal with the inner connection between natural phenomena and living reality in the world, and you have already seen that there are many things of which those whose vision is limited to the world of outward appearance have no idea. We have seen how every species of living being—this was shown by a number of examples—has its task in the whole nexus of cosmic existence. Now today, as a kind of recapitulation, we will again consider what I said recently about the nature of several creatures and in the first place of the butterfly. In my description of butterfly nature, as contrasted with that of the plants, we found that the butterfly is essentially a creature that belongs to the light—to the light in so far as it is modified by the forces of the outer planets, of Mars, Jupiter and Saturn. Hence, if we wish to understand the butterfly in its true nature, we must look up into the higher regions of the cosmos, and must say to ourselves: 'These higher cosmic regions endow and bless the earth with the world of the butterflies.'

The bestowal of this blessing upon the earth has an even deeper significance. Let us recall how we had to say that the butterfly does not participate in anything directly connected with earthly existence, but only indirectly, in so far as the sun, with its power of warmth and light, is active in this earthly existence. Actually a butterfly lays its eggs only where they do not become separated from sun activity, so that the butterfly does not entrust its egg to the earth, but only to the sun. Then the caterpillar emerges; it is under the influence of Mars activity, though naturally the sun influence always remains. The chrysalis develops under the influence of Jupiter activity. From it emerges the butterfly, whose iridescent colours reflect in the earth's environment the luminous sun power that the earth can potentially evolve in conjunction with the power of Saturn.

Thus in the manifold colours of the butterfly world we see the direct effect of Saturn activity in earth existence and in the earth's environment. But let us bear in mind that the substances necessary for earth existence are in fact of two kinds. We have the purely material substances of the earth, and we have the spiritual substances; and I told you that the remarkable thing about this is that in the case of man the underlying substance of his metabolism and limbs is spiritual whereas that of the head is physical. Moreover in man's lower nature spiritual substance is permeated with the activity of physical forces, with the action of gravity, with the action of the other earthly forces. In the head, earthly substance, conjured up into it by the whole of metabolism, circulation, nerve activity and the like, is permeated by non-physical spiritual forces, which are reflected in our thinking, in our power of forming mental images. Thus in the human head we have spiritualized physical matter and in the limbs and metabolism we have en-earthed—if I may coin a word—en-earthed spiritual substantiality.

Now it is spiritualized matter that we find to the greatest degree in the butterfly. Because a butterfly always remains in the sphere of sun existence, it only takes to itself earthly matter—naturally I am still speaking figuratively—as though in the form of the finest dust. It also gets its nourishment from earthly substances that have been worked through by the sun. It unites with its own being only what is sun-imbued; and it takes from earthly substance only what is finest, and works on it until it is entirely spiritualized. When we look at a butterfly's wing we actually have before us earthly matter in its most spiritualized form. Through the fact that the physical substance of the butterfly's wing is imbued with colour, it is the most spiritualized of all earthly substances.

The butterfly is the creature which lives entirely in spiritualized earth matter. And the spiritual eye is able to perceive that in a certain way a butterfly despises the body which it carries between its coloured wings because its whole attention, its whole group soul being, is centred on joyous delight in the colours of its wings.

And just as we marvel at its shimmering colours as we follow it, so also can we marvel at its own fluttering joy in these colours. This is something which it is of fundamental importance to cultivate in children, this joy in the spirituality fluttering about in the air, which is in fact fluttering joy, joy in the play of colours. The nuances of butterfly nature reflect all this in a wonderful way; and something else lies in the background as well.

We were able to say of the bird—which we regarded as represented by the eagle—that at its death it can carry spiritualized earth substance into the spiritual world, and that thereby, as a bird, it has the task in cosmic existence of spiritualizing earthly matter, thus being able to accomplish what cannot be done by man. Human beings have earth matter in their heads that has also been spiritualized to some degree, but they cannot take this earthly matter into the world in which they live between death and a new birth for they would continually have to endure unspeakable, unbearable, devastating pain if they were to carry this spiritualized earth matter of the head into the spiritual world.

The bird world, represented by the eagle, can do this, so that a connection is actually created between what is earthly and what is extra-earthly. Earthly matter is, as it were, gradually transformed into spirit, and bird creation has the task of giving over this spiritualized earthly matter to the universe. One can actually say that when the earth has reached the end of its existence, this earth matter will have been spiritualized, and that bird creation had its place in the whole economy of earthly existence for the purpose of taking this spiritualized earth matter back into spirit land.

It is somewhat different with butterflies. The butterfly spiritualizes earthly matter to an even greater degree than the bird. The bird after all is much closer to the earth than the butterfly. I will explain this in detail later. Because the butterfly never actually leaves the region of the sun, it is in a position to spiritualize its matter to such a degree that it does not, like the bird, have to await its death, but even in life is continually restoring spiritualized matter to the environment of the earth, to the cosmic environment of the earth.

Only think of the magnificence of all this in the whole cosmic economy! Picture the earth with the world of the butterflies fluttering around it in its infinite variety, continually sending out into world space the spiritualized earthly matter which this butterfly world yields up to the cosmos! Then, with such knowledge, we can contemplate the region of the butterfly world which encircles the earth with totally different feelings.

We can look into this fluttering world and say: From you, O fluttering creatures, there streams out something even better than sunlight; you radiate spirit light into the cosmos! Our materialistic science pays but little heed to things of the spirit and those who work with it therefore simply do not have the means of grasping these things, which are, nevertheless, part of the whole cosmic economy. They are there, just as the effects of physical activities are there, and they are even more real. For what thus streams out into spirit land will work on further when the earth has long passed away, whereas what is taught by the modern chemist and physicist will reach its end with the conclusion of the earth's existence. So that if some observer were to sit outside in the cosmos, with a long period of time for observation, he would see something like a continual outstreaming into spirit land of matter which has become spiritualized, as the earth radiates its own being out into cosmic space; and he would see—like scintillating sparks that ever and again flash up into light—what the bird kingdom, what every bird after its death sends forth as glittering light, streaming out into the universe in the form of rays: a shimmering of the spirit light of the butterflies, and a sparkling of the spirit light of the birds.

Such things as these should also make us realize that when we look up to the rest of the starry world, we should not think that from there, too, there only streams down what is shown by the spectroscope, or rather what is conjured into the

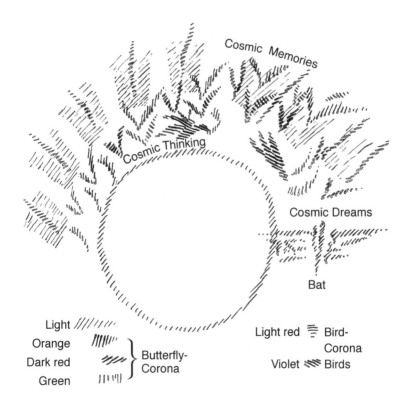

Cosmic Memories

Cosmic Thinking

Cosmic Dreams

Bat

Light ///////
Orange
Dark red
Green
} Butterfly-
Corona

Light red ≡ Bird-
Corona
Violet ≋ Birds

spectroscope by the fantasy of the scientist using it. What streams down to earth from other worlds of the stars is just as much the product of living beings as what streams out from the earth into world space is the product of living beings. People look at a star, and with the modern physicist picture it as something in the nature of an inorganic flame that has been lit—or something like that. This, of course, is absolute nonsense. For what we behold there is entirely the product of something imbued with life, imbued with soul, imbued with spirit.

And now let us pass inwards from this girdle of butterflies—if I may call it so—which encircles the earth, and return to the kingdom of the birds. If we call to mind something which is already known to us, we must picture three regions adjoining each other. (There are other regions above these, and again other regions below them.) We have the light ether and we have the heat ether, which however actually consists of two parts, of two layers, the one being the layer of heat from the earth, the other that of cosmic heat, and these continually play one into the other. Thus we have not only one, but two kinds of heat, the one which is of earthly, tellurian origin, and the other of a kind which is of cosmic origin. These are always playing one into the other. Then bordering on the heat ether, there is the air. Below this would come water and earth, and above would come chemical ether and life ether.

The world of the butterflies belongs more particularly to the light ether; it is the light ether itself which is the means whereby the power of the light draws forth the caterpillar from the butterfly's egg. Essentially it is the power of the light which draws the caterpillar forth.

This is not the case with the bird kingdom. The birds lay their eggs. These must now be hatched out by warmth. The butterfly's egg is simply given over to what is of the nature of the sun; the bird's egg comes into the region of warmth. It is in the region of the heat ether that the bird has its being, for it actually overcomes what is purely of the air.

The butterfly, too, flies in the air, but fundamentally it is entirely a creature of the light. And as the air is permeated with light, the butterfly chooses not air but light existence within this light-and-air existence. To the butterfly the air is only what sustains it—the waves, as it were, on which it floats; but the butterfly's real element is the light. The bird flies in the air, but its element is the warmth in the air, the various temperature differentiations, and to a certain degree it overcomes the air. Inwardly, too, the bird is to a high degree an air being. The bones of mammals and of human beings are filled with marrow. (We shall speak later of why this is the case.) The bones of a bird are hollow and are filled only with air. We consist, in so far as the content of our bones is concerned, of what is of the nature of marrow; a bird consists of air. And what is of the nature of marrow in us is simply air in the bird. If you take the lungs of a bird, you will find a whole quantity of sacs which project from the lungs; these are air sacs. When a bird inhales it does not only breathe air into its lungs, but it breathes the air into these air sacs, and from there the air passes into the hollow bones. So that, if one could remove from the bird all its flesh and all its feathers and also take away the bones, one would still have a creature composed of air, having the form of what inwardly fills out the lungs, and what inwardly fills out all the bones. Visualizing this purely as a form, you would actually get the form of a bird. Within the eagle of flesh and bone dwells an eagle of air. This is not only because within the eagle there is also an eagle of air, but the bird also breathes and through its breathing it produces heat. This it imparts to the air in its body, pushing it into its entire limb system. Thus arises the difference in temperature as compared to its outer environment. The bird has its internal body temperature, as against the temperature in the surrounding atmosphere. In this difference of degree between the temperature of the outer air and the temperature which the bird imparts to its own air within itself—it is really in this that the bird lives and has its being. And if you could find a way of asking a bird how matters stand with its body, the bird's reply would make you realize, providing you understood bird language, that it regards its solid physical bones, and other material adjuncts, rather as you would regard luggage, as if you were loaded down with suitcases on the left and the right, on your back and head. You would not call this luggage your body. In the same way the bird, in speaking of itself, would only speak of the air to which it has given warmth as its body, and of everything else as the luggage which it carries about with it in earthly existence. The bones that envelop the real body of the bird are its luggage. We are therefore certainly able to say that fundamentally the bird lives only and entirely in the element of warmth, and the butterfly in the element of light. For the butterfly everything of the nature of physical substance, which it spiritualizes, is, before it is spiritualized, not even personal luggage but more like furniture. It is even more remote from its real being.

When we thus ascend to the creatures of these regions, we come to something which cannot be judged in a physical way. If we do judge it physically, it is rather as if we were to draw a person with his hair grown into the bundle he is carrying on his head, suitcases grown together with his arms, and his back with whatever he is carrying on his back—such as a rucksack—making him appear a perfect hunchback. If one were to draw a person in this way, it would actually correspond to the materialist's view of the bird. That is not the bird; it is the bird's luggage. The bird really feels encumbered by having to drag its luggage about, for it would like best to pursue its way through the world free and unencumbered, as a creature of warm air. For the bird all else is a burden. And the bird pays its dues to world existence by spiritualizing this burden for it, sending it out into spirit land when it dies; while the butterfly already pays these dues during its lifetime.

You see, a bird breathes and makes use of the air in the way I told you. It is otherwise with the butterfly. The butterfly does not in any way breathe by means of an apparatus such as the so-called higher animals possess (they are simply more bulky and not really higher). The butterfly breathes in fact only through tubes which pass inwards from the outside of its body. These are somewhat dilated, so that it can store air during flight and is not inconvenienced by always having to breathe. The butterfly always breathes through tubes which pass into its interior. Because this is so, it can take up into its whole body, together with the air which it inhales, the light which is in the air. Here, too, a great difference is to be found.

Let us represent this in a diagram. Picture to yourselves one of the higher animals, one with lungs. Into the lungs comes oxygen, and there it unites with the blood in its passage through the heart. In these more bulky animals, and also in man, the blood must flow into the heart and lungs in order to come in contact with oxygen.

In the case of the butterfly I must draw the diagram quite differently, in this way: If this is the butterfly, the tubes go in everywhere; they branch out inside. And the oxygen enters in everywhere, and spreads itself out through the tubes; the air penetrates into the whole body.

With us, and with the so-called higher animals, the air comes as far as the lungs as air only; in the case of the butterfly the outer air is dispersed into the whole interior of the body with its content of light. The bird diffuses the air right into its hollow bones; the butterfly is not only a creature of light outwardly, but it diffuses the light which is carried by the air into every part of its entire body, so that inwardly too the butterfly is composed of light. Just as I could characterize the bird as warmed inner air, so in fact is the butterfly composed entirely of light. Its body also consists of light; and for the

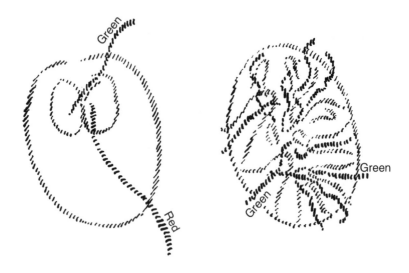

butterfly warmth is actually a burden, its luggage. It flutters about only and entirely in the light, and it is light only that it builds into its body. When we see butterflies fluttering in the air, we should really see them only as fluttering creatures of the light rejoicing in their play of colours. All else is garment, is luggage. We must gain an understanding for what the creatures in the environment of the earth really consist of, for outward appearance is deceptive.

People today who have superficially learned this or that of Oriental wisdom speak of the world as maya. But to say that the world is maya really implies nothing. One must have insight into the details of why it is maya. We understand maya when we know that the real nature of the bird in no way accords with what is to be seen outwardly, but that it is a creature of warm air. The butterfly is not at all what it appears to be, but what is seen fluttering about is a creature of the light, a creature that essentially consists of joy in the play of colours. This arises on the butterfly's wings through earthly dust substance being imbued with the element of colour and thus entering the first stage of its spiritualization on a passage out into the spiritual universe, into the spiritual cosmos.

You see, we have here, as it were, two levels: the butterfly, the inhabitant of the light ether in the earth environment, and the bird, the inhabitant of the warmth ether in the earth environment. And now comes the third level. When we descend to the level of the air, we come to the creatures that actually could not have existed at a certain period of our earth evolution; for instance at the time when the moon had not yet separated from the earth but was still within it. Here we come to creatures that are certainly also creatures of the air, for they live in the air, but are in fact already strongly influenced by gravity, which is peculiar to the earth. The butterfly is completely untouched by earth's gravity. It flutters joyfully in the light ether, and feels itself to be a creature of that ether. The bird overcomes gravity by imbuing the air within it with warmth, thereby becoming a creature of warm air—and warm air is upborne by cold air. It still overcomes earth's gravity.

The creatures that by reason of their origin must still live in the air but are unable to overcome earth's gravity, because they have not hollow bones but bones filled with marrow, and also because they do not have air sacs like the birds—these creatures are the bats.

Bats are a quite remarkable order of animal life. In no way do they overcome the gravity of earth through what is inside their bodies. They do not, like the butterflies, possess the weightlessness of light, or, like the bird, the lightness of warmth; they are subject to earth's gravity, and they experience themselves in their flesh and bone. Hence that element of which the butterfly consists, which is its whole sphere of life—the element of light—is disagreeable to bats. They like the twilight. Bats have to make use of the air, but they like the air best when it is not the bearer of light. They yield themselves up to the twilight. They are veritable creatures of the twilight. And bats can only maintain themselves in the air because they possess their somewhat caricature-like bat wings, which are not wings at all in the true sense, but membranes stretched between their elongated fingers, a kind of parachute. By means of these they maintain themselves in the air. They overcome gravity by opposing to it a counter-weight that in itself is related to gravity. Through this, how-ever, they are completely yoked into the domain of earth forces. One could never construct the flight of a butterfly solely according to physical, mechanical laws, nor could one do this for the flight of a bird. Things would never come out absolutely right. In their case we must introduce something involving other laws of construction. But you can certainly construct the bat's flight according to earthly dynamics and mechanics.

The bat does not like the light, the light-imbued air, but at the most only twilight air. And the bat also differs from the bird through the fact that the bird, when it looks about it, always has in view what is in the air. Even the vulture, when it steals a lamb, perceives it as though it were at the end of the air sphere; looking down it sees the lamb as if it were something painted on to the earth. And quite apart from this, it is no mere act of seeing; it is desire. What you would perceive if you took a proper look at the flight of the vulture directed towards the lamb is a veritable dynamic of intention, of volition, of desire.

A butterfly sees everything that is on the earth as though in a mirror; to the butterfly the earth is a mirror for what is in the cosmos. When you see a butterfly in the air, you have to realize that it ignores the earth, for it is just a mirror reflecting the cosmos. A bird does not see what belongs to the earth, but it sees what is in the air. The bat is the first of these creatures to perceive what it flies through, or flies past. And because it does not like the light, it is unpleasantly affected by everything it sees. It can certainly be said that the butterfly and the bird see in a very spiritual way. The first creature—descending from above downwards—that has to see in an earthly way, is disagreeably affected by this seeing. A bat dislikes seeing, and in consequence it has a kind of embodied anxiety, a fear of what it sees but does not want to see. And so it would like to flit past everything. It is obliged to see, yet is unwilling to do so—and thus it tries just to skirt past everything. And it is because it desires just to slip past everything, that it is so wonderfully intent on listening. The bat is actually a creature which is continually listening to its own flight, lest this flight should be in any way endangered.

Only look at the bat's ears. You can see from them that they are attuned to world fear. So they are—these bat's ears. They are quite remarkable structures, attuned to going softly through the world, attuned to world fear and anxiety. All this, you see, is only to be understood when the bat is studied in the context into which we have just placed it.

Here we must add something further. The butterfly continually imparts spiritualized matter to the cosmos. It is the darling of the Saturn influences. Now call to mind how I described Saturn as the great bearer of the memory of our planetary system.* The butterfly is closely connected with the capacity for memory in our planet. It is memory-thoughts which live in the butterfly. The bird—this, too, I have already described—is entirely a head, and as it flies through the warmth-imbued air in world space it is actually a thought in living flight. What we have within us as thoughts—and this also is connected with the warmth ether—is bird nature, eagle nature, in us. The bird is the flying thought. But the bat is the flying dream; the flying dream picture of the cosmos. So we can say: The earth is surrounded by fluttering butterflies— they are cosmic memory; by the kingdom of the birds—this is cosmic thinking; and by the bats—they are cosmic dream,

---

* See 'The Spiritual Individualities of the Planets', a lecture given by Rudolf Steiner in Dornach on 27 July 1923. Published in *The Golden Blade* 1966.

cosmic dreaming. The flying dreams of the cosmos actually rush through space as bats. And as dreams love the twilight, so, too, does the cosmos love the twilight and send the bat through space. The enduring thoughts of memory, these we see embodied in the girdle of butterflies encircling the earth; thoughts of the moment we see in the birds encircling the earth; and dreams in the environment of the earth fly about embodied as bats. And you will surely feel, if you enter deeply enough into their form, how much affinity there is between looking at a bat in this way and having a dream! One simply cannot look at a bat without the thought arising: I must be dreaming; that is really something which should not be there, something which is as much outside the other creations of nature as dreams are outside ordinary physical reality.

So we can say: The butterfly sends spiritualized substance into spirit land during its lifetime; the bird sends it out after its death. Now what does the bat do? During its lifetime the bat gives off spiritualized substance, especially that spiritualized substance which exists in the stretched membrane between its separate fingers. But it does not give this over to the cosmos; it sheds it into the atmosphere of the earth. Thereby beads of spirit, so to say, are continually produced in the atmosphere.

Thus we find the earth to be surrounded by the continual glimmer of outstreaming spirit matter from the butterflies, and sparkling into this what comes from the dying birds; but also, radiating back towards the earth, we find peculiar forms enclosed in the air where the bats give off what they spiritualize. Those are the spiritual formations which are always to be observed when one sees a bat in flight. In fact a bat always has a kind of tail behind it, like a comet. The bat gives off spirit matter; but instead of sending it outwards, it thrusts it back into the physical substance of the earth. It thrusts it back into the air. And just as one sees with the physical eye physical bats fluttering about, one can also see these corresponding spirit formations which emanate from the bats rushing through the air; they rush through the spaces of the air. We know that air consists of oxygen, nitrogen and other constituents, but this is not all; it also consists of the spirit emanations of bats.

Strange and paradoxical as it may sound, this dream order of the bats send little spectres out into the air, which then unite into a single mass. In geology the matter below the earth, which is a rock mass of a soft consistency like porridge, is called magma. We might also speak of a spirit magma in the air, which comes from the emanations of bats.

In ancient times when an instinctive clairvoyance prevailed, people were very susceptible to this spirit magma, just as today many people are susceptible to what is of a more material nature, for instance, bad smells. This might certainly be regarded as something more common and ordinary, whereas in the ancient instinctive time of clairvoyance people were susceptible to the bat residue which is present in the air.

They protected themselves against this. And in many of the mysteries there were special formulas whereby people could inwardly shut themselves off, so that this bat residue might have no power over them. For as human beings we do not only inhale oxygen and nitrogen with the air, we also inhale these bat residues. Modern people, however, are not interested in protecting themselves against these bat residues, for whereas in certain conditions they are highly sensitive, let us say, to bad smells, they are highly insensitive to the bat residues. It can really be said that they swallow them down without feeling the least trace of repulsion. It is quite extraordinary that people who are otherwise quite fussy just swallow down what contains the stuff of which I have spoken. Nevertheless this too enters into the human being. It does not enter into the physical or ether body, but it enters into the astral body.

Yes, you see, we here find remarkable connections. Initiation science everywhere leads into the inner aspect of relationships; this bat residue is the most desirable food of what I have described in lectures here as the Dragon. But this bat residue must first be breathed into the human being. The Dragon finds his surest foothold in human nature when man allows his instincts to be imbued with these bat-emanations. There they seethe. And the Dragon feeds on them and grows fat—in a spiritual sense, of course—gaining power over people, gaining power in the most manifold ways. This is something against which modern man must again protect himself; and the protection should come from what has been described here as the new form of Michael's fight with the Dragon. The increase in inner strength which man gains when he takes up into himself the Michael impulse as it has been described here in Dornach, this is his safeguard against the food that the Dragon desires; this is his protection against the bat residue that is wrongfully in the atmosphere.

If one has the will to penetrate into these inner cosmic connections, one must not shrink from facing the truths contained in them. For today the generally accepted form of the search for truth does not in any way lead to anything real, but at most to something even less real than a dream, to maya. Reality must of necessity be sought in the domain where all physical existence is regarded as interwoven with spiritual existence. We can only find our way to reality if we look at it the way it is now being done in these lectures.

Everything good and everything evil is in some way or other connected with beings that are to be found somewhere. Everything is part of the great cosmic scheme of things and its connection with other beings can be recognized. For the materialistically minded, butterflies flutter, birds fly, bats flit. But this can really be compared to what often happens with a not very artistic person who adorns the walls of his room with all manner of pictures which do not belong to each other, which have no inner connection. Thus for the ordinary observer of nature, what flies through the world also has no inner connection; because he sees none. But everything in the cosmos has its own place, because from this place it has an inner relationship to the cosmos in its totality. Be it butterfly, bird, or bat, everything has its own meaning within the world order.

As to those who today wish to scoff, let them scoff. Other things may be more worthy of ridicule. In the past, experts from renowned academic institutions declared that meteoric rocks could not exist because iron could not fall from heaven, and so on. Why then should people not also scoff at the functions of the bats about which I have spoken today? Such things, however, should not divert us from the task of imbuing our civilization with a knowledge of spiritual truths.

Lecture 6

28 October 1923

Before we proceed to the study of the other members of the animal, plant and mineral kingdoms, which are connected with man, we must first cast a glance at the development of man himself, and call to mind various descriptions already familiar to us through books or lectures. This will give us the necessary overview.

If we look to present-day science for instruction, we are usually told that it is necessary to investigate how the so-called higher forms of the plant, animal and human kingdoms have evolved out of lifeless, so-called inorganic substances or forces.

A true conception of evolution reveals something essentially different. It reveals—as you will have been able to gather from my *Occult Science*—that man in his present form is the being who has the longest evolution behind him, an evolution that goes back to the time of ancient Saturn. We must therefore say that man is the oldest creature within the evolution of our earth. It was only during the Sun period that animal nature was added, then during the Moon period plant nature; and the mineral kingdom, as we know it today, is in fact an earth product, something which was only added during the Earth period of evolution.

Let us now consider man in his present form and ask ourselves: What part of man evolved earliest? It is the human head. This first evolved at a time when the earth was in its Saturn metamorphosis. It is true that ancient Saturn consisted entirely of heat substance, and the human head was then actually flowing, moving, surging heat; it then acquired gaseous form during the Sun period, and fluid-form during the Moon period, when it became a liquid, flowing entity; and only during the Earth period did it receive the solid form with its bony parts. We must therefore say that a being of which it is difficult to gain a conception through today's external forms of knowledge existed during the time of ancient Saturn, and of this being the human head is the descendant. And simultaneously with the formation of man's head—this can be gathered from my recent descriptions—simultaneously with the first beginnings of the human head during the Saturn period, the first beginnings of butterfly nature also came into existence. Later we shall make a more exact study of the nature of the other insects, but to begin with let us stay with butterfly nature. When we follow the course of evolution from the ancient Saturn period until today, until earth existence, we must say that at that time the beginnings of the human head came into existence in a form of very delicate substance; and at the same time there arose everything which now flutters through the air as the world of the butterflies.

The two evolutionary paths proceeded further. Man developed his inner being so that to an ever greater degree he manifested a soul nature and radiated outward from within. The butterfly, on the other hand, is a being on whose exterior the cosmos may be said to lavish all its beauties. The butterfly is a creature on which everything of beauty and majesty in the cosmos—as this has been described to you—has, as it were, alighted together with the dust on its wings. We must, therefore, picture butterfly nature as a mirror which reflects the beauties of the upper cosmos. The human being takes up into himself, encloses within himself, what is of the nature of the upper cosmos, and thus becomes inwardly ensouled. It is like a concentration of the cosmos which then radiates outwards, giving form to itself in the human head, so that in the

human head we have something formed from within outwards. But in the butterfly we have something formed from
outside in. Someone who sees these things with the eye of
vision learns something really tremendous if he sets to work in
the following way. He says: I wish to fathom the mysteries, the
most ancient mysteries, the Saturn mysteries of the human
head; I wish to know the true nature of the forces that have
held sway inside the skull. He must then let his attention be
directed to what is everywhere to be seen outside, to what
everywhere streams inwards from outside. To come to know
the marvel that is your own head, study the marvels of how the
butterfly came to be in the world of nature outside. This is the
great lesson imparted by a study of the cosmos through
spiritual observation.

Evolution then proceeded from the Saturn period to the
Sun period, and now a being came into existence possessed of
a further development, an air development, an air metamorphosis, of the head; but to this there was added in very delicate
substance what later became the organs of the chest, became
the breathing apparatus and the heart of man. In Saturn we
still have essentially the metamorphosis that represents the
human head. When we come to the Sun period we have the
head and chest; for it was now that the part was added which
today is the human chest. At the same time, however, there
already came into existence, in the later part of the Saturn
period and the earlier part of the Sun period, what must now
be seen as having its representative in the eagle. The bird
kingdom arose in the first part of the Sun period, and in the
second part of the Sun period there arose the first rudiments
of that kingdom of the animals which are in fact chest animals,
as, for instance, the lion—other chest animals, too, but the
lion as their representative. So that the first beginnings of
these animals go back to the time of old Sun.

From this you can see what a stupendous difference exists
when it comes to the evolution of even the higher animals and

of man. In the future I shall still have to speak about the transitional animals, which include the apes,* but today my intention is just to give a comprehensive overview. You see what an immense difference exists between the development of man and the development of the higher animals.

In the case of human evolution it was the head which first took form. All the other organs are, as it were, appended; they may be said to have attached themselves to the formation of the head. In cosmic evolution man's development proceeds from the head downwards. On the other hand the lion, for example, first came into existence during the old Sun period as a chest animal, as an animal with a powerful breathing system, but with a head still very small and poorly developed. And only in later times when the sun separated from the earth and then worked from outside, only then did the head develop out of the chest. Thus the development of the lion was such that it evolved from the chest upwards, whereas the human being evolved from the head downwards. This constitutes an immense difference in evolution as a whole.

And when we now proceed to the Moon metamorphosis of the earth, because the Moon represented the water condition, because the Moon was fluid—though it certainly developed a hornlike substance in its later period—it was only then that the human being needed a further extension downwards. The beginnings of the digestive system developed. During the old Sun period, while man possessed only what was of the nature of air, undulating, scintillating with light, all he required for the purpose of nourishment was a breathing apparatus shut off from below; man was a head-and-breathing organism. Now, during the Moon period, he acquired a digestive system, thereby becoming a being of head, chest and abdomen. And because everything in the old Moon was still watery substance,

* See for example Steiner's lecture of 6 August 1924 in *The Evolution of the Earth and Man.* Anthroposophic Press, New York 1987.

the human being had outgrowths during this old Moon period which buoyed him up as he swam through the water. We can only speak of arms and legs during the Earth period, when the force of gravity took effect, and the part developed that is primarily aligned to the lines of gravity—the limbs. This, therefore, belongs only to the Earth period. During the Moon period, however, the digestive system was formed, though still quite differently constituted from what it was to be later on; for man's digestive apparatus did not as yet need to assimilate all that serves the free, independent mobility of the limbs. It was still an essentially different digestive system; this was later metamorphosed into the digestive apparatus appropriate to the earth. It was, however, during the Moon period that man first acquired his digestive system.

And then it came about that to the descendants of the butterflies, of the birds and of such species as are represented by the lion, were added the animals that are predominantly designed for digestion. Thus, during the Moon period we have the addition of the animals that are represented by the cow.

How then did the development of the cow proceed in contrast to that of the human being? Here matters were such that in this old Moon period it was first and foremost the cow's digestive apparatus that evolved; then, after the moon had separated, the chest organs grew out from the digestive system, as did also the characteristically shaped head. Man began his development with the head, adding to this the chest, and finally the digestive organs; the lion began with the chest organs, adding to these the head, and then, during the old Moon period, acquiring the digestive organs at the same time as man did; the animals represented by the cow had first, as a primary beginning, the digestive organs, and then growing out from these the organs of the chest and head. So you see, man grew from the head downwards, the lion from the chest both upwards and downwards; the cow grew from its digestive organs into the chest and head, so that compared to the human being it grew entirely in an upward direction and developed towards heart and head. That is what we see when we consider the evolution of the human being.

Here the question naturally arises: Is it only the cow which was, one can say, the companion thus associated with man's evolution? This is not entirely so, for whenever any kind of planetary metamorphosis takes place, the earlier creatures develop further, while at the same time new ones come into existence. The cow already came into being during the first phase of Moon metamorphosis. Then, however, other animals were added, and these had their very earliest beginning in the last phase of the Moon metamorphosis. These could not, for example, take part in the departure of the moon, for it had already separated off. Nor could they participate in what this departure brought about, namely, the drawing forth, as it were, from the cow's belly of the organs of heart and head. The creatures which made their appearance later remained at the stage which in man is focused in digestion, the stage which man carries with him in his abdomen.

And just as the eagle and the butterflies are constituted in relation to the head, the lion in relation to the chest, the cow in relation to the abdomen (though it was also able to develop all the upper organs at a later period of evolution), so the amphibians and reptiles, such as toads, frogs, snakes, lizards, are related, if I may put it so, to the lower organs of the human being, those of the human digestive system. They are simply digestive organs which came into existence as animals.

BUTTERFLIES	BIRDS. LIONS	COWS. REPTILES. AMPHIBIANS
		FISHES
Saturn	*Sun*	*Moon*
Head	Head-Chest	Head-Chest-Abdomen

These last creatures appeared during the second Moon period in an extremely clumsy-looking form, and were in fact walking stomachs and entrails, walking stomachs and intestinal tubes. And only later, during the earth period, did they also acquire a still not particularly distinguished-looking head system. Just look at frogs and toads, or at snakes. They came into existence as animals of digestion at a late period, at a time when man could only append his digestive apparatus to what he had already acquired during an earlier period.

And in the Earth period, when man acquired his limbs under the influence of gravity and earth magnetism, the tortoises—we may take the tortoises as representative animals in this—stretched their head out beyond their armoured shell in a manner more like an organ of the limb system than a head. And now we can understand how it is that in the case of the amphibians and reptiles the head is formed in such an uncouth way. Its form is such that one really has the feeling—and rightly so—that here one passes directly from the mouth into the stomach. There is hardly anything in between.

When we study man in this way and relate his animal companions to the different aspects of his nature, we must assign what is comprised in the reptiles and amphibians to the human activity of digestion. And one can actually say: Just as man carries around in his intestines the products of his digestion, so does the cosmos carry around—indirectly by way of the earth—toads, snakes and frogs in the cosmic intestine which it created for itself in the watery-earthly element of the earth. On the other hand, all that is more connected with human reproduction, which appeared in its earliest beginnings in the very last phase of the Moon period and only developed fully during the earth metamorphosis, with this the fishes are related, the fishes and still lower animals. So that we have to regard the fishes as late arrivals in evolution, as creatures that only joined the company of the other animals at a time when man added his organs of reproduction to those of digestion. The snake is the intermediary between the organs of reproduction and digestion. Rightly viewed in regard to human nature, what does the

snake represent? It represents what is known as the renal
tubule; it originated in world evolution at the same time as the
renal tubule developed in man.

Thus we can actually follow the way the human being,
beginning with the head, grew downwards, how the earth
drew forth from him the limbs and made them its servants, so
that these limbs are within the earth equilibrium of gravity and
magnetic forces. And simultaneously with this downward
growth the different classes of the animals took form.

You see, this gives us a true picture of the evolution of the
earth and its creatures. And in accordance with this evolution
these creatures have developed in such a way that they present
themselves to us as they are today. When you look at the
butterflies and the birds you certainly have earthly forms; but
you know from what has been said before that the butterfly is
really a light being and earthly substance has, as it were, only
alighted on it. If the butterfly itself could tell you what it is, it
would announce to you that it has a body made of light, and
that, as I have already said, it carries about what has alighted
on it in the way of earthly matter like luggage, like something
external to itself. Similarly one can say that the bird is a
creature of warm air, for the true bird is the warm air that is
diffused throughout its body; all else is its luggage which it
carries with it through the world. These creatures, which even
today have still preserved their nature of light and warmth,
and are really only clothed with a terrestrial, an earthly, a
watery vestment, were the very earliest to arise in the whole of
earth evolution. Their very forms can remind anyone who is
able to look back to the time which man passed through in the
spiritual world, before his descent into earthly life, of occur-
rences in the spiritual world. Certainly they are earthly forms,
for earthly matter has alighted on them.

If we conceive rightly the hovering, swooping creature of
the light that is the real butterfly, thinking away everything of
an earthly nature which has alighted on it; if we think away

from the bird everything of earth which has alighted on it; if we picture the assembly of forces which makes of the bird a creature of warm air, with its plumage in reality just shining rays; if we imagine all this, then these creatures (which only look as they do and are the size they are because of their outer vestment) remind the seer who knows what the nature of the human being was before the descent to earth, of that human descent. Then one who can thus gaze into the spiritual world says to himself: The butterflies and the birds remind us of the spirit-forms among which man dwelt before he descended to earth, of the beings of the higher hierarchies. Looked at with understanding, butterflies and birds are a memory—transformed into miniature and metamorphosed—of the forms that man had around him as spirit-forms before he descended into earth evolution. Because earth substance is heavy and must be overcome, the butterflies contract into miniature the gigantic form which is in reality theirs. If you could separate from a butterfly everything of the nature of earth substance, it would be able, as spirit-being, as a creature of the light, to expand to archangelic form. In the creatures that inhabit the air we have the earthly images of spiritual forms that exist in higher regions. This is why, in the time of instinctive clairvoyance, it was the natural thing in artistic creation to derive from the forms of the winged creatures the symbolic form, the pictorial form, of the beings of the higher hierarchies. This has its inner justification. Essentially the physical forms of butterflies and birds are really the physical metamorphoses of spiritual beings. It is not the spiritual beings themselves which have undergone metamorphosis, but these forms are their metamorphosed images; they are of course different beings.

You will, therefore, also find it understandable that I return to something which I have already discussed and I again draw what follows in a diagram.* I told you that the butterfly, which

---

* See page 75.

is essentially a creature of the light, continually sends spiritualized earth matter out into the cosmos during its lifetime. I'd like to call this spiritualized earth substance which is sent out into the cosmos—borrowing a term customary in solar physics—the butterfly corona. That is how the butterfly corona continually radiates out into the cosmos. But into this butterfly corona radiates what the bird kingdom yields up to the cosmos every time a bird dies, so that the spiritualized matter from the bird kingdom radiates into the corona and out into the cosmos. Thus in spiritual perception one beholds a shimmering corona emanating from the butterfly kingdom—certain laws allow this to continue in winter also—and in a more ray-like form, introduced into it, one beholds what streams out from the birds.

You see, when the human being has the impulse to descend from the spiritual world to the physical world, it is the butterfly corona, this remarkable outstreaming of spiritualized earth substance, which first calls him into earthly existence. And the rays of the bird corona are experienced more as forces that enter into the corona. Now you perceive an even higher significance in what has its life in the encircling air. We must look for the spiritual in everything that is alive and active within reality. And it is only when one looks for the spiritual that one comes to the significance of various different species and spheres of being. The earth entices man back into incarnation by sending forth into world space the shining radiance of the butterfly corona and the rays of the bird corona.* These call man back again into a new earthly existence after he has spent a certain period of time between death and rebirth in the purely spiritual world. It is, therefore, not to be wondered at if man finds it difficult to unravel the complex feelings which he

---

* See the words of the Neophyte in Scene 8 of Rudolf Steiner's mystery play *The Soul's Awakening.* Published in *Four Mystery Dramas.* Rudolf Steiner Press, London 1997.

rightly experiences when beholding the world of the butterflies and the birds. For the true reality of these dwells deep in the subconscious. What really works in them is the remembrance of a longing for new earthly existence.

This again is connected with something I have often spoken of, namely, that the human being, when he has departed from the earth through the portal of death, actually disperses his head, and that then the remainder of his organism—naturally in regard to its forces, not in regard to its matter—becomes metamorphosed into the head of his next earthly existence. Thus man is striving towards his head when he is striving towards his descent. And it is the head which is the first part of the human embryo to develop in a form which already resembles the later human form. All this has to do with the fact that this directing of development towards the head is intimately connected with what works and moves in the world of the flying creatures, by means of which man is drawn out of supersensible into sensible existence.*

The human being therefore first acquires his head organization during the embryonic period; after this the digestive organization, and so forth, develops out of earthly existence and it does so inside the mother's body. Just as the upper part, the development of the head, is connected with what is of the nature of warmth and air, with the warmth-light element, so what is now added during the embryonic period is connected with the element of earth and fluid; it follows the same pattern as the parts appended during the later stages of human evolution. The element of earth and fluid must, however, be prepared in a quite special way and this has to be in the mother's body. If it evolved separately, scattered over the

---

* See also Rudolf Steiner's lecture on 'Cosmic Formative Forces in Relation to the Hierarchies' (Dornach, 16 July 1921; German in GA 205). Translation published in *Anthroposophical Movement* 1931: vol 8, Supplement 7.

earthly world outside, it would develop into lower animal forms such as amphibians and reptiles, or into fishes and even lower animals.

The butterfly rightly regards itself as a creature of the light, the bird as a being of warm air, but this is impossible for the lower animals—amphibians, reptiles and fishes. Let us first consider the fishes as they are today, as they come into existence subject to external forces that work on them from the outside, whereas they work on man from inside. A fish lives primarily in the element of water. But water is certainly not just the combination of hydrogen and oxygen which it is for the chemist. Water is permeated by all kinds of cosmic forces. Stellar forces also enter into it. No fish would be able to live in water if it were merely a homogeneous combination of hydrogen and oxygen. Just as the butterfly feels itself to be a creature of the light, and the bird a creature of warm air, so the fish feels itself to be a creature of earth and water. It does not feel the actual water which it absorbs to be part of its own being.

A bird does feel the air which it inhales to be part of its own being. Thus the bird actually feels the air that enters into it

and is everywhere diffused through it, as its own being; this air which is diffused through the bird and warmed by it, this is its being. The fish has water within it, yet it does not feel itself to be water; the fish feels itself to be what encloses the water, what surrounds the water. It feels itself to be the glittering shell or vessel enclosing the water. But the water itself is felt by the fish to be an element foreign to it, which passes in and out, and, in doing so, also provides the air which the fish needs. Yet air and water are felt by the fish as something foreign. In its physical nature the fish experiences the water as something foreign to it. But the fish also has its ether and astral bodies. And it is just this which is the remarkable thing about the fish. Because it really experiences itself as vessel, and feels that the water this vessel encloses remains connected with all the rest of the watery element, the fish experiences the ether to be the element in which it actually lives. It does not feel the astral as something belonging to it.

Thus the fish has the peculiar characteristic that it is so entirely a creature of the ether. It feels itself as the physical vessel for the water. It feels the water within itself as part and parcel with all the waters of the world. Fluid continues on into every part of it, as it were. Fluid is everywhere, and in this wetness the fish at the same time experiences the ether. For earthly life fishes are certainly dumb, but if they could speak and could tell you what they feel, they would say: 'I am a vessel, but the vessel contains the all pervading element of water, which is the bearer of the element of ether. I am really swimming in the ether.' The fish would say: 'Water is only maya; the reality is the ether, and it is in this that I really swim.' Thus the fish feels its life to be at one with the life of the earth. This is the peculiar thing about the fish: it feels its life as the life of the earth, and therefore takes an intimate part in everything which the earth experiences during the course of the year, experiencing the outgoing of the etheric forces in summer, the withdrawing of etheric forces in winter. The fish experiences something which breathes within the whole earth. The fish perceives the etheric element as the breathing process of the earth.

Dr Wachsmuth once spoke here about the breathing of the earth.* This was a very beautiful description. If a fish had learned the art of lecturing, it could have given the very same lecture here out of its own experience, for it perceives everything that was described in this lecture from having itself participated in all the phenomena in question! The fish is the creature which takes part in quite an extraordinary way in the breathing life of the earth during the cycle of the year, because what is important for the fish is the element of life, the ether that surges out and in, drawing all other aspects of breathing with it.

It is otherwise with the reptiles and with the amphibians; with the frogs, for instance, which are remarkably characteristic in this respect. They are not so much connected with the ether in the cosmos; they are connected more with the astral element. If one were to ask a fish: 'What, exactly, is your situation?' it would answer: 'Well, yes, here on earth I have become an earthly creature, made out of the element of earth and water; but my real life is the life of the whole earth with its cosmic breathing.' This is not so with the frog; here matters are essentially different. The frog shares in the astrality that is to be found everywhere.

In regard to the plants I told you—and I shall speak further of this—how the astrality of the cosmos touches the flower. The frog is connected with this astrality, with what may be called the astral body of the earth, just as the fish is connected with the earth's ether body. The fish possesses its astrality more for itself. The frog possesses its ether body very much for itself, much more so than the fish; but the frog lives in the

---

* Dr Guenther Wachsmuth. *Die ätherischen Bilderkräfte in Kosmos, Erde und Mensch.* Stuttgart 1924.

general astrality; it shares particularly in the astral processes that occur in the cycle of the year, when the earth brings its astrality into play in the evaporation of water and its recondensation. Here the materialistically-minded person naturally says that the evaporation of water is caused by aerodynamic, or, if you will, aero-mechanical forces of one kind or another; these cause the ascent. Drops are formed, and when they become heavy enough they fall downwards. But this is almost as though one were to put forward a similar theory about the circulation of the human blood without taking into consideration the fact that everything is full of life in the circulation of the blood. In the same way the astral atmosphere of the earth, the earth's astrality, lives in the circulation of water as it goes up and comes down again. And I am telling you no fairytale when I say that it is just the frogs—this is also the case with the other amphibians, but to a less pronounced degree— that live in this play of astrality which manifests in weather conditions, in meteorology. It is not only that frogs are used— as you know—in a simple, easy way to foretell the weather, but they experience this astral play so wonderfully because their own astrality places them right into the astrality of the earth. The frog does not even say: 'I have a feeling'; it is merely the bearer of the feelings that the earth has in wet spells, in dry spells, and so on. This is also why in certain weather conditions you have the more or less beautiful (or ugly) frogs' concerts. For this is the frogs' way of expressing what they experience in conjunction with the astral body of the earth. They actually do not croak unless they are moved to do so by what comes from the whole cosmos; they live with the astrality of the earth.

So we can say that the creatures that live in the element of earth and moisture also have more of a living experience of the earth: earthly life conditions in the case of the fish and earthly feeling conditions in the case of the frog—and reptiles and amphibians in general. Again, if we wish to study the human digestive organism, we must say that it has developed from within and on this particular pattern. However, if we really wish to study how it functions, we must turn to the world of amphibians and reptiles, for the forces with which the human being imbues his digestive apparatus comes to them from outside. The same forces by means of which man digests are used by the outer cosmos, by outer nature, to produce snakes, toads, lizards and frogs. And whoever wishes to make a real study—forgive me, but there is nothing ugly in nature, everything must be considered objectively—whoever wishes to study the inner nature of, let us say, the human colon with its powers of excretion, must study the toads in outer nature; for there comes to the toads from outside what works in the same pattern but from within outwards in the human colon. Certainly this does not lend itself to such beautiful descriptions as what I had to say about the butterflies; but everything in nature must be viewed with objective impartiality.

In this way, you see, you also gain a picture of how the earth shares in the life of the cosmos. Turn your attention to what may be called the earth's excretory organs; the earth excretes not only the nearly lifeless products of human excretion, but it also excretes what is living, and among its actual excretions are the toads. In them the earth rids itself of what it is unable to use.

From all this you can see how outer nature always corresponds to what is within us. Anyone who says: 'No mind has been created that penetrates the inner life of nature,'* simply does not know that the inner life of nature is to be found everywhere in the outside world. We can study the entire human being in regard to his inner nature, if we understand what is alive and active outside in the cosmos. We can study the human being from head to limb system if we study what is

---

*Johann Wolfgang von Goethe, in 'Freundlicher Zuruf'. See Rudolf Steiner's *Goethe the Scientist*. Anthroposophic Press, New York 1950.

present in the outside world. World and man belong together in every respect. And one can even represent this in a diagram. We draw the circumference or periphery of a large circle; its power is concentrated in a point. The periphery gives rise to a smaller circle inside; the point at the centre radiates outwards to create the same form. The smaller periphery in turn generates an even smaller circle; the power inside again radiates outward to create the same form. The new periphery creates a further one; and again the human being radiates outwards. Thus the outer aspect of the human being comes into contact with the inner nature of the cosmos. At the point where our senses come in contact with the world, the part of us that has gone out from the inner centre comes in contact with what in the cosmos has entered from the periphery. In this sense man is a small world, a microcosm in relation to the macrocosm. But he contains all the wonders and secrets of the macrocosm, only in a reversed evolutionary direction.

It would be something very adverse to the further evolution of the earth if things were only as I have so far described them; then the earth would excrete the toads and would one day perish just as physical man must perish, without any continuation. So far, however, we have only considered man's connection with the animals, and have built only a tentative bridge to plant nature. We shall now have to penetrate further into the plant world, and then into the mineral world, and we shall see how the mineral world arose during the Earth period—how, for instance, the rock formations of our primary mountains were laid down, bit by bit, by the plants, and how, bit by bit, the limestone mountains were laid down by the animals that came later. The mineral kingdom is the deposit of the plant and animal kingdom, and it is mainly the deposit of the lowest animals. The toads do not contribute very much to the mineral element of the earth; the fishes, too, comparatively little; but the lower animals and the plants contribute a very great deal. The lower creatures, those plated with siliceous and calcareous armour or calcareous shells, deposit what they have first created out of their own animal— or plant—natures, and the mineral then disintegrates. And when this mineral substance disintegrates, a power of the highest order takes hold of just these products of mineral disintegration and from them builds up new worlds. The mineral element in any particular place can become of all things the most important.

When we follow the course of earth evolution—heat state, airy state, watery state, mineral earthly state—the human head has participated in all these metamorphoses, the mineral metamorphosis initially on the outside, in the decaying skeleton of the head—though this still retains a certain vitality. But the human head has participated in the earthly mineral metamorphosis in a way which is even more apparent. In the centre of the human head within the structure of the brain there is an organ shaped like a pyramid, the pineal body. This gland, situated in the vicinity of the superior colliculi (corpora quadrigemina) and the optic thalamus secretes out of itself the so-called brain sand, minute lemon-yellow stones which lie in little heaps at one end of the pineal body, and which are truly the mineral element in the human head. If they do not lie there, if a human being does not have this brain sand, this mineral element, within him, he becomes mentally retarded. In the case of normal people the pineal body is comparatively large. In the mentally retarded, pineal bodies have been found which are actually no larger than hemp seeds; these cannot secrete brain sand.

It is actually in this mineral deposit that the spirit-man is anchored; and this immediately shows that what is living cannot harbour the spirit, but that the spirit in man needs something non-living as its centre, which means that above all else it must be a spirit with independent life.

A beautiful progression has taken us from butterfly and

head development and bird and head development all the way down to the reptiles and fishes. We will now re-ascend and study what will give us as much satisfaction as the succession of animals—the succession of plants and that of minerals. And just as we have been able to learn about the past from the succession of animals, so shall we be able to derive hope for the future of the earth from the succession of minerals. At the same time it will of course still be necessary in the following lectures to enter into the nature of transitional animals from the most varied aspects, for in this survey I have only been able to touch on the animals of principal significance, which, so to say, appear at the key points of evolution.

Part Three

The Plant World and the Elemental Nature Spirits

'The World Word is not some combination of syllables gathered from a limited number of sources; the World Word is the harmony of what sounds forth from a countless multitude of beings.'

Lecture 7

2 November 1923

To the outwardly perceptible, visible world there belongs the invisible world, and these, taken together, form a whole. The marked degree to which this is the case first appears in its full clarity when we turn our attention away from the animals to the plants.

Plant life, as it sprouts and springs forth from the earth, immediately arouses our delight, but it also provides access to something which we must feel to be full of mystery. In the case of the animal, though certainly its will and whole inner activity have something of the mysterious, we nevertheless recognize that this will is actually there, and is the cause of the animal's form and outer characteristics. But in the case of the plants, which appear on the face of the earth in such magnificent variety of form, which develop in such a mysterious way out of the seed with the help of earth and the surrounding air—in the case of the plant we feel that some other factor must be present in order that this plant world may arise in the form it does.

When spiritual vision is directed to the plant world, we are immediately led to a whole host of beings which were known and recognized in the old times of instinctive clairvoyance but which were afterwards forgotten and today remain only as names used by the poet, names to which modern man ascribes no reality. To the same degree, however, in which we deny reality to the beings that flit so busily around the plants, to that degree do we lose understanding of the plant world.

This understanding of the plant world, which, for instance, would be so necessary for the practice of medicine, has been entirely lost to present day humanity.

We have already recognized a very significant connection between the world of plants and the world of butterflies; but this too will only really come alive for us when we look yet more deeply into the whole range of activities and processes that go on in the plant world.

Plants send down their roots into the ground. Anyone who can observe what they really send down and can perceive the roots with spiritual vision (for this he must have) sees how the root is everywhere surrounded by the activities of elemental nature spirits. And these elemental spirits, which an old clairvoyant perception designated as gnomes and which we may call the root spirits, can actually be studied through Imagination and Inspiration,* just as human life and animal life can be studied in the physical world. We can look into the soul nature of these elemental spirits, into this world of the spirits of the roots.

The root spirits are quite special earth folk, invisible at first to outer view, but in their effects so much the more visible; for no root could develop if it were not for what is mediated between the root and the earth realm by these remarkable root spirits, which bring the mineral element of the earth into flux in order to conduct it to the roots of plants. I am of course referring to the underlying spiritual process.

These root spirits, which are everywhere present in the earth, get a quite particular sense of well-being from rocks and from ores (which may be more or less transparent and also

---

* Imagination, Inspiration and Intuition are three perceptive faculties developed on the anthroposophical path of knowledge. Rudolf Steiner described these and ways of achieving them on many occasions. See his *Occult Science. An Outline*. Rudolf Steiner Press, London 1979; a clear exposition is also given in his *Fruits of Anthroposophy*. Rudolf Steiner Press, London 1986.

contain metallic elements). They have the greatest feeling of well-being in this sphere because it is the place where they belong, where they are conveying what is mineral to the roots of the plants. And they are filled with an inner spirituality that we can only compare to the inner spirituality of the human eye and the human ear. For these root spirits are in their spiritual nature entirely sense. Apart from this they are nothing at all; they consist only of sense. They are entirely sense, and it is a sense which is at the same time *intellect*, which does not only see and hear, but immediately understands what is seen and heard; it not only receives impressions, but everywhere also receives ideas.

We can even indicate the way in which these root spirits receive their ideas. We see a plant sprouting out of the earth. The plant enters, as I shall presently show, into connection with the extra-terrestrial universe; and, particularly at certain seasons of the year, spiritual currents flow from above, from the flower and the fruit of the plant down into the root, streaming into the earth. And just as we turn our eyes towards the light and see, so do the root spirits turn their faculty of perception towards what trickles downwards from above, through the plant into the earth. What trickles down towards the root spirits is something which the light has sent into the flowers, which the heat of the sun has sent into the plants, which the air has produced in the leaves, which the distant stars have brought about in creating the plant form. The plant gathers the secrets of the universe, sends them into the ground, and the gnomes take these secrets into themselves from what trickles down spiritually to them through the plants. And because the gnomes, particularly from autumn on and through the winter, in their wanderings through ore and rock, bear with them what has trickled down to them through the plants, they are the beings within the earth which carry the ideas of the whole universe on their streaming, wandering journey through the earth.

We look out into the wide world. The world has been built of the spirit of the universe; it embodies the ideas of the universe, of the spirit of the universe. Through the plants, which to them are the same as rays of light are to us, the gnomes take in the ideas of the universe and carry them in full consciousness from metal to metal, from rock to rock within the earth.

We gaze down into the depths of the earth, not to seek there below for abstract ideas about some kind of mechanical laws of nature, but to behold the roving, wandering gnomes, which are the light-filled preservers of cosmic reason within the earth.

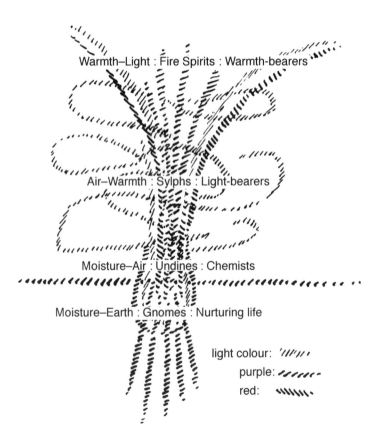

Warmth–Light : Fire Spirits : Warmth-bearers

Air–Warmth : Sylphs : Light-bearers

Moisture–Air : Undines : Chemists

Moisture–Earth : Gnomes : Nurturing life

light colour:

purple:

red:

These gnomes have immediate understanding of what they see; their knowledge is of a similar nature to that of man, but they are the epitome of intellect, they are nothing but intellect. Everything about them is intellect, but an intellect so universal that they look down on human reason as something imperfect. The gnomes laugh us to scorn on account of the groping, struggling intellect with which we manage to grasp one thing or another, whereas they have no need at all to think things out. They have direct perception of what is sensible and intelligent in the world; and they are particularly ironical when they notice the efforts people have to make to come to this or that conclusion. Why should they do this? say the gnomes—why ever should people give themselves so much trouble to think things over? We *know* everything we look at. People are so stupid, say the gnomes, for they must first think things over.

Gnomes can actually be ironical to the point of ill manners if one speaks to them of logic. For why ever should people need such a superfluous thing—a training in thinking? The thoughts are already there. The ideas flow through the plants. Why don't people stick their noses into the earth down to the depth of the plant's roots, and let what the sun says to the plants trickle down into their noses? Then they would know something! But with logic—say the gnomes—one can only have odd bits and pieces of knowledge.

Thus the gnomes are actually the bearers of the ideas of the universe, of the cosmos, inside the earth. But for the earth itself they have no liking at all. They flit about in the earth with cosmic ideas, but they actually hate what is earthly. This is something from which the gnomes would best like to escape. Nevertheless they remain with the earthly—you will soon see why this is so—but they hate it, for the earthly threatens them with continual danger. The earth continually holds over them the threat of forcing them to take on particular shapes, the configuration of the creatures I described to you in the last lecture, the amphibians, and in particular of frogs and toads. The feeling of the gnomes within the earth is really this: If we grow too strongly together with the earth, we shall assume the form of frogs or toads. They are continually on the alert to avoid being caught up too strongly in the earth and be forced to take on such an earthly form. They are always on the defensive against this earthly form, which threatens them in the element in which they exist as I have described. They have their home in the element of earth and moisture; there they live under the constant threat of being forced into amphibian forms. From this they continually tear themselves free by filling themselves entirely with ideas of the extra-terrestrial universe. The gnomes are really the element within the earth which represents the extra-terrestrial, because they must continually avoid growing together with the earthly; otherwise they would individually take on the forms of the amphibian world. And it is just from what I may call this feeling of hatred, this feeling of antipathy towards the earthly, that the gnomes gain the power of driving the plants up from the earth. With the fundamental force of their being they unceasingly thrust away from the earthly, and it is this thrust that determines the upward direction of plant growth; they impel the plants along with them. The antipathy that the gnomes have to anything earthly causes the plant to have only its roots in the earth and then grow out of the earth; in fact, the gnomes force the plants out of their true, original form and make them grow upwards and out of the earth.

Once the plant has grown upwards, once it has left the domain of the gnomes and has passed out of the sphere of the element of moist earth into the sphere of moist air, the plant develops what comes to outer physical form in the leaves. Other beings are at work now in everything that goes on in the leaves—water spirits, elemental spirits of the watery element, to which an earlier instinctive clairvoyance gave the name of undines, among others. Just as we found gnome beings flitting busily around the roots, we see close to the soil these water beings, these elemental beings of the water, these undines, who observe with pleasure the upward-striving growth that the gnomes have produced.

These undine beings differ in their inner nature from the gnomes. They cannot turn outwards towards the universe like a spiritual sense organ. They can only yield themselves up to the movement and activity of the whole cosmos in the element of air and moisture and they therefore do not have the clarity of mind that the gnomes have. They dream incessantly, these undines, but their dream is at the same time their own form. They do not hate the earth as intensely as do the gnomes, but they have a sensitivity to what is earthly. They live in the etheric element of water, swimming and floating in it. They are highly sensitive to anything in the nature of a fish; for the fish's form is a threat to them. They do assume it from time to time, though only to forsake it immediately in order to take on another metamorphosis. They dream their own existence. And in dreaming their own existence they bind and release, they bind and separate the substances of the air, which in a mysterious way they introduce into the leaves. They take these substances to the plants that the gnomes have thrust upwards. The plants would wither at this point if it were not for the undines, who approach from all sides, and as they move around the plants in their dream-like consciousness, they prove to be what we can only call world chemists. The undines dream the binding and releasing of substances. And this dream, through which the plant exists, into which it grows when, developing upwards, it leaves the ground, this undine dream is the world chemist inducing the mysterious combining and separation of substances in the plant world, starting in the leaf. We can therefore say that the undines are the chemists of plant life. They dream of chemistry. They possess an exceptionally delicate spirituality which is really in its element just where water and air come into contact with each other. The undines live entirely in the element of moisture, but they feel their own inner satisfaction when they come to the surface of something watery, be it only a drop of water or something else of a watery nature. For their whole endeavour lies in preserving themselves from totally assuming the form of a fish, the permanent form of a fish. They wish to remain in a state of metamorphosis, in a state of eternal, endlessly continuing changeability. But in this state of changeability, in which they dream of the stars and of the sun, of light and of heat, they become the chemists who now, starting from the leaf, continue with the further development of the plant form that has been thrust upwards by the gnomes. So the plant develops its leaf growth, and this mystery is now revealed as the dream of the undines into which the plants grow.

To the same degree, however, in which the plant grows into the dream of the undines, it now enters into another domain higher up, into the domain of the spirits which live in the element of air and warmth, just as the gnomes live in that of earth and moisture and the undines in the element of air and moisture. In the element of air and warmth live the beings which an earlier clairvoyant faculty called the sylphs. Because air is everywhere imbued with light, these sylphs living in the element of air and warmth press towards the light and become related to it. They are particularly susceptible to more delicate but more widespread movements within the atmosphere.

When in spring or autumn you see a flock of swallows, which produce vibrations in a body of air as they fly along, creating a current of air, this moving air current—and this holds good for every bird—is something the sylphs can hear. Cosmic music is what they hear from it. If, let us say, you are travelling somewhere by ship and the seagulls are flying towards it, their flight sets in motion spiritual sounds, a spiritual music that accompanies the ship.

Again it is the sylphs which unfold and develop their being within this sounding music, finding themselves at home in the moving current of air. It is in this spiritually sounding, moving element of air that they find themselves at home; and at the same time they absorb what the power of light sends into these vibrations of the air. Because of this the sylphs, which experience existence more or less in a state of sleep, feel most in their element, most at home, where birds are winging through the air. If a sylph is obliged to flit through air devoid of birds, it feels as though it had lost itself. But at the sight of a bird in the air something quite special comes over the sylph. I have often had to describe a certain event in human life, the event which leads the human soul to address itself as 'I'. And I have always drawn attention to the statement made by Jean Paul: that, when a human being first arrives at the conception of his 'I', it is as though he looks into the most deeply veiled Holy of Holies of his soul. A sylph does not look into any such veiled Holy of Holies of its own soul, but when it sees a bird a feeling of ego comes over it. The sylph feels its ego through what the bird sets in motion as it flies through the air. And because this is so, because its ego is kindled in it from outside, the sylph becomes the bearer of cosmic love through the atmosphere. It is because the sylph embodies something like a human wish, but does not have its ego within itself but in the bird kingdom, that it is at the same time the bearer of wishes of love through the universe.

Thus we behold the deepest sympathy between the sylphs and the bird world. The gnome hates the amphibian world, the undine is sensitive to fishes, is unwilling to approach them, seeks to avoid them and feels a kind of horror for them. The sylph, on the other hand, is attracted towards birds, and has a sense of well-being when it can waft towards their feathered flight the floating air filled with sound. And were you to ask a bird from whom it learns to sing, you would hear that its inspirer is the sylph. Sylphs feel a sense of pleasure in the bird's form. They are however prevented by the cosmic order from becoming birds, for they have another task. Their task is lovingly to convey light to the plant. And just as the undine is the chemist for the plant, so is the sylph the light bearer. The sylph imbues the plant with light; it bears light into the plant.

Through the fact that the sylphs bear light into the plant, something quite remarkable is brought about. You see, the sylph is continually carrying light into the plant. The light, that is to say the power of the sylphs in the plant, works on the chemical forces that were induced in the plant by the undines. Here occurs the interworking of the sylph's light and the undine's chemistry. This is a remarkable moulding and shaping activity. With the help of the upstreaming substances which are worked on by the undines, the sylphs weave an ideal plant form out of the light. They actually weave the Archetypal Plant within the plant from light and from the chemical working of the undines. And when towards autumn the plant withers and everything of physical substance disperses, then these forms of the plants begin to trickle downwards, and now the gnomes perceive them, perceive what the world—the sun through the sylphs, the air through the undines—has brought to pass in the plant. This the gnomes perceive, and throughout the entire winter they are engaged in perceiving below what has trickled down into the soil from the plants. Down there they grasp world ideas in the plant forms which have been given shape and form with the help of the sylphs, and which now enter into the soil in their spiritual, ideal form.

People who regard the plant as something material will of course know nothing of this spiritual ideal form. Thus at this point a colossal error, a terrible error appears in materialistic observation of the plant. I'll give you a brief outline of this.

Everywhere you will find that in materialistic science matters are described as follows: The plant takes root in the ground, above the ground it develops its leaves and finally its

flowers, and within the flower the stamens, then the carpel.*
The pollen from the anthers—usually from another plant—is
taken over to the stigma, the carpel is fertilized and through
this the seed of the new plant is produced. That is the usual
way of describing it. The carpel is regarded as the female
element and what comes from the stamens as the male—
indeed matters cannot be regarded otherwise as long as
people remain bound to materialism, for then this process
really does look like fertilization. This, however, it is not. In
order to gain insight into the process of fertilization, that is to
say the process of reproduction, in the plant world, we must
be conscious that in the first place the plant form arises
through the work of those great chemists, the undines, and the
work of the sylphs. This is the ideal plant form which goes
down into the ground and is kept safely by the gnomes. It is
there below, this plant form. And there within the earth it is
now guarded by the gnomes after they have seen and perceived it. The earth becomes the womb for what thus trickles
downwards. This is something quite different from what is
described in materialistic science.

Up here (see drawing), after it has passed through the
sphere of the sylphs, the plant enters the sphere of elemental
fire spirits. These inhabit the element of heat and light. When
the warmth of the earth is at its height, or has reached a suf-
ficient level, it is gathered up by the fire spirits. Just as the
sylphs gather up the light, so do the fire spirits gather up the
warmth and carry it into the flowers of the plant.

Undines carry the action of chemical ether into the plants,
sylphs the action of light ether into the flowers. And the pollen
provides what may be called little airships that enable the fire

---

* A structure at the heart of the flower, consisting of the ovary containing
the ovules, and the style bearing the stigma. In botanical works usually
referred to as 'the female reproductive organ of flowering plants'.—
Translator.

spirits to carry warmth into the seed. Everywhere warmth is collected with the help of the stamens, and is carried by means of the pollen from the anthers to the seeds in the carpel. And what is formed here in the carpel in its entirety is the male element that comes from the cosmos. It is not a case of the carpel being female and the anthers of the stamens being male. In no way does fertilization occur in the flower, but only the preforming of the male seed. Fertilization occurs when the cosmic male seed, which fire spirits in the flower take from the warmth of the universe, is brought together with the female principle that has trickled down into the soil as an ideal element at an earlier stage, as I have described, and is resting there.

For plants the earth is the mother, the heavens the father. And all that takes place outside the domain of the earth is not the maternal womb for the plant. It is a colossal error to believe that the maternal principle of the plant is in the carpel. This is in fact the male principle which has been drawn forth from the universe with the aid of the fire spirits. The maternal element is taken from the cambium of the plant, which lies between bark and wood, and carried down as ideal form. And what now results from the combined gnomes' and fire spirits' activity—this is fertilization. The gnomes are, in fact, the spiritual midwives of plant reproduction. Fertilization takes place below in the earth during the winter, when the seed enters the earth and meets with the forms which the gnomes have received from the activities of the sylphs and undines, and which they now carry to where these forms can meet with the fertilizing seeds.

You see, because people do not recognize what is spiritual, do not know that gnomes, undines, sylphs and fire spirits— which were formerly called salamanders—are actively involved in plant growth, there is a complete lack of clarity about the process of fertilization in the plant world. Up there, outside the earth, nothing by way of fertilization takes place; the earth is the mother of the plant world, the heavens the father. This is the case in a quite literal sense. Plant fertilization takes place through the fact that gnomes take from fire spirits what the fire spirits have carried into the carpel as concentrated cosmic warmth on the tiny airships of the anther pollen. Thus the fire spirits are the bearers of warmth.

And now you will easily gain insight into the whole process of plant growth. First, with the help of what comes from the fire spirits, the gnomes down below instil life into the plant and push it upwards. They are the fosterers of life. They carry the life ether to the root—the same life ether in which they themselves live. The undines foster the chemical ether in the plant, the sylphs the light ether, the fire spirits the warmth ether. And then the fruit of the warmth ether again unites with what is present below as life. Thus plants can only be understood when they are considered in connection with all that is flitting around them full of life and activity. And one only reaches the right interpretation of the most important process in the plant when one penetrates into these things in a spiritual way.

When once this has been understood, it is interesting to look again at the words Goethe jotted down when responding to another botanist—he was terribly annoyed because people talked about endless 'marriages' going on in the plants. Goethe was affronted by the idea that constant marriages were being consummated all over every meadow. This seemed to him something unnatural. In this Goethe had an instinctive but very true feeling. He could not as yet know the real facts of the matter, but nevertheless his instinct was a sure one. He could not see why fertilization should take place up there in the flower. He did not as yet know what goes on below ground and that the earth is the maternal womb of the plants. But he instinctively knew that the process which takes place in the flower is not what all botanists take it to be.*

You are now aware of the inner connection between plant and earth. But here is something else which you must take into account.

You see, when up above the fire spirits are flitting around the plant and transmitting the pollen from the anthers, they have only one feeling which, compared to the feeling of the sylphs, they have in an enhanced degree. The sylphs experience their self, their ego, when they see the birds flit about. The fire spirits have this experience, but to an intensified degree, in regard to the butterfly world and indeed the insect

---

* 'Endless marriages'—Goethe jotted down the words: 'Study dispersal through pollen, evaporation, dispersal in droplets'. See *Goethe the Scientist* (op. cit.).

world as a whole. And it is these fire spirits which take the utmost delight in following in the tracks of the insects' flight so that they convey warmth to the carpel. In order to carry the concentrated warmth, which must descend into the earth so that it may be united with the plant's ideal form, the fire spirits feel themselves intimately related to the butterfly world, and to the world of the insects in general. Everywhere they follow in the tracks of the insects as they flit from flower to flower.*
And so one really has the feeling, when following the flight of insects, that each of these insects as it flits from flower to flower, has a quite special aura which cannot be entirely explained from the insect itself. Particularly the luminous, wonderfully radiant, shimmering aura of bees, as they flit from flower to flower, is unusually difficult to explain. And why? It is because the bee is everywhere accompanied by a fire spirit which feels so closely related to it that, for spiritual vision, the bee is surrounded by an aura which is actually a fire spirit. When a bee flies through the air from plant to plant, from tree to tree, it flies with an aura that is actually given to it by a fire spirit. The fire spirit does not only gain a feeling of its ego in the presence of the insect, but it wishes to be completely united with the insect.

Through this, insects also obtain that power about which I have spoken to you, which even shows itself in a shimmering forth of light into the cosmos. They obtain the power completely to spiritualize the physical matter which unites itself with them, and to allow this spiritualized physical substance to ray out into cosmic space. But just as heat is what first causes light to shine, so, above the surface of the earth, when the insects bring about this shimmering forth into cosmic space—which attracts the human being to descend again into physical incarnation—it is the fire spirits which inspire the

---

* See Ariel's Song in *The Tempest* by William Shakespeare: 'Where the bee sucks, there suck I . . .' (Editor's note).

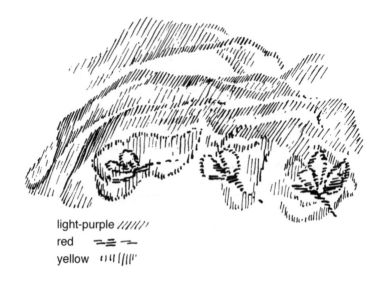

light-purple //////'
red   ‒‑‑ ‑‑
yellow   ιιιιι ι|||ι'

insects to this activity, the fire spirits that flit around them. But if the fire spirits are active in promoting the outstreaming of spiritualized matter into the cosmos, they are no less actively engaged in seeing to it that the concentrated fiery element, the concentrated warmth, goes into the interior of the earth; so that with the help of the gnomes the spirit form, which sylphs and undines cause to trickle down into the earth, may be awakened.

This, you see, is the spiritual process of plant growth. And it is because the subconscious in man divines something of a special nature in the flowering, sprouting plant that he experiences the being of the plant as full of mystery. This is not to dismantle the mystery, of course, nor brush the dust from the butterfly's wings. Our instinctive delight in the plant is raised to a higher level when not only the physical plant is seen, but also that wonderful working of the gnomes' world below, with its immediate understanding that gives rise to intelligence, the gnomes' world which first pushes the plant upwards. Just as the human intellect is not subject to gravity, but the head is carried without us feeling its weight, so the gnomes with the light of their intellect overcome what is of the earth and push the plant upwards. They prepare life down below. But the life would die away were it not given impetus by the chemical activity brought to it by the undines. And this must be imbued with light.

And so we picture, from below upwards, in bluish, blackish shades the force of gravity, to which an upward impulse is given by the gnomes; and flitting all around the plant—indicated by the leaves—the undine power that blends and disperses substances as the plant grows upwards. From above downwards, from the sylphs, light is made to leave its imprint in the plant and moulds and creates the form which descends as an ideal form and is taken up by the maternal womb of the

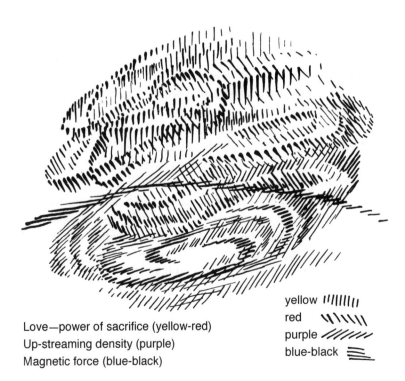

yellow ‖‖‖‖‖

red ＼＼＼＼

purple ⁄⁄⁄⁄⁄

blue-black ≋

Love—power of sacrifice (yellow-red)

Up-streaming density (purple)

Magnetic force (blue-black)

earth; moreover fire spirits flit around the plant and concentrate cosmic warmth in the tiny seed points. This is sent down to the gnomes together with the seed power, so that down there they can cause the plants to arise out of fire and life.

And further we now see that essentially the earth is indebted for its power of repulse and impulse for growth, and its density, to the antipathy of the gnomes and undines towards amphibians and fishes. If the earth is dense, this density is due to the antipathy by means of which the gnomes and undines maintain their form. When light and warmth come down to earth, this is at the same time an expression of that power of sympathy, that sustaining power of sylph love, which is carried through the air, and to the sustaining sacrificial power of the fire spirits, which brings the power to descend to what is below. So we may say that, over the face of the earth, earth density, earth magnetism and earth gravity, in their upwardly striving aspect, unite with the downward striving power of love and sacrifice. And in this interworking of the downwards streaming force of love and sacrifice and the upwards streaming force of density, gravity and magnetism, in this interworking, where the two streams meet, plant life develops on the surface of the earth. Plant life is an outer expression of the interworking of world love, world sacrifice, world gravity and world magnetism.

So now you have seen what matters when we direct our gaze to the plant world, which so enchants, uplifts and inspires us. Real insight can only be gained when our vision embraces the spiritual, the supersensible, as well as what is accessible to the physical senses. This enables us to correct the capital error of materialistic botany, that fertilization occurs above the earth. What occurs there is not the process of fertilization, but the preparation of the plant's heaven-born male seed for the future plant being nurtured in the maternal womb of the earth.

Lecture 8

3 November 1923

Yesterday I spoke to you about the other side of the natural world, about the supersensible and invisible beings which accompany the beings and processes visible to the senses. An earlier, instinctive vision beheld the beings of the supersensible world as well as those in the world of the senses. Today, these beings have withdrawn from human view. The reason why this company of gnomes, undines, sylphs and fire spirits is not perceptible in the same way as animals, plants and so on, is merely that man, in the present epoch of his earth evolution, is not in a position to unfold his soul and spirit without the help of his physical and ether bodies. In the present situation of earth evolution man is obliged to depend on the etheric body for the purposes of his soul, and on the physical body for the purposes of his spirit. The physical body which provides the instrument for the spirit, that is, the sensory apparatus, is not able to enter into communication with the beings that exist behind the physical world. It is the same with the etheric body, which man needs to develop as an ensouled being. Through this, if I may put it so, half of his earthly environment escapes him. He passes over everything connected with the elemental beings about which I spoke yesterday. The physical and the ether body have no access to this world. We can gain an idea of what actually escapes human beings today when we realize what such gnomes, undines, and so on, actually are.

We have, you see, a whole host of lower animals—lower at

the present time—animals that consist only of a soft mass, live in the fluid element, and have nothing in the way of a skeleton to give them internal support. They are creatures which belong to the latest phase of the earth's development; creatures which only now, when the earth has already evolved, develop what man—the oldest earth being—already developed in his head structure during the time of ancient Saturn. These creatures have not progressed to the stage of producing the hardened substance in them that can become supporting skeleton.

It is the gnomes which, in a spiritual way, make up in the world for what is lacking in the lower orders of the animals up to the amphibians, and fish, which have only the beginnings of a skeleton. These lower animal orders only become complete, as it were, through the fact that gnomes exist.

The relationships between beings in the world are very different, and something arises between these lower creatures and the gnomes which I yesterday called antipathy. The gnomes do not wish to become like these lower creatures. They are continually on the watch to protect themselves from assuming their form. As I described to you, the gnomes are extraordinarily clever, intelligent beings. With them intelligence is already implicit in perception; they are in every respect the antithesis of the lower animal world. And whereas they have the significance for plant growth which I described yesterday, in the case of the lower animal world they actually provide its complement. They supply what this lower animal world does not possess. This lower animal world has a dull consciousness; the gnomes have a consciousness of the utmost clarity. The lower creatures have no bony skeleton, no bony support; the gnomes bind together everything that exists by way of gravity and fashion their bodies from this volatile, invisible force, bodies which are, moreover, in constant danger of disintegrating, of losing their substance. The gnomes must ever and again create themselves anew out of gravity, because they continually stand in danger of losing their substance. Because of this, in order to save their own existence, the gnomes are constantly attentive to what is going on around them. No being is a more attentive observer on earth than a gnome. It takes note of everything, for it must know everything, grasp everything, in order to preserve its existence. A gnome must always be wide awake; if it were to become sleepy, as people often do, this sleepiness would immediately cause its death.

There is a German saying of very early origin which aptly expresses this characteristic of the gnomes, in having always to remain attentive. People say: Look sharp like a goblin. And the gnomes are goblins. So, if one wishes to make someone attentive, one says to him: Look sharp like a gnome. A gnome is really an attentive being. If one could place a gnome as an object lesson on a front desk in every school classroom, where all could see it, it would be a splendid example for the children to follow.

The gnomes have yet another characteristic. They are filled with an absolutely unconquerable lust for independence. They trouble themselves little about one another and give their attention only to the world of their own surroundings. One gnome takes little interest in another. But everything else in this world around them, in which they live, this interests them exceedingly.

Now I told you that the human body really is a hindrance to our perceiving such folk as these. The moment it ceases to be this hindrance, these beings are there, just as the other beings of nature are there for ordinary vision. Anyone who gets to the stage of experiencing his dreams in full consciousness on falling asleep is well acquainted with the gnomes. You need only recall what I recently published in the *Goetheanum* on the subject of dreams.* I said that a dream in no way appears to

---

* Rudolf Steiner. *On the Life of the Soul.* Anthroposophic Press, New York 1985.

ordinary consciousness in its true form, but wears a mask. Such a mask is worn by the dream that we have on falling asleep. We do not immediately escape from the experience of our ordinary day consciousness. Reminiscences well up, memory pictures from life; or we perceive symbols representing the internal organs—the heart as a stove, the lungs as wings—all in symbolic form. These are masks. If someone were to see a dream unmasked, if he were actually to pass into the world of sleep without the beings existing there being masked, then, at the moment of falling asleep, he would behold a whole host of goblins coming towards him.

In ordinary consciousness man is protected from seeing these things unprepared, for they would terrify him. The form in which they would appear would actually be reflections, images of all the qualities in the individual concerned that work as forces of destruction. He would perceive all the destructive forces within him, all that continually destroys. These gnomes, if perceived unprepared, would be nothing but symbols of death. Man would be terribly alarmed by them, if in ordinary consciousness he knew nothing about them, and was now confronted by them on falling asleep. He would feel entombed by them—for this is how it would appear—entombed by them yonder in the astral world. For, seen from the other side, what takes place on falling asleep is a kind of entombment by gnomes.

This holds good only for the moment of falling asleep. A further complement to the physical, sense-perceptible world is given by the undines, the water beings, which continually transform themselves, and which live in connection with water just as the gnomes live in connection with the earth. These undines—we have come to know the role they play in plant growth—exist as complementary beings to animals that are at a somewhat higher stage and have assumed a more differentiated earthly body. These animals, which have developed into the more evolved fishes, or also into the more evolved amphibians, require scales, require some sort of hard external armour. For the powers needed to provide certain creatures with this outer support, this outer skeleton, the world is indebted to the activity of the undines. The gnomes spiritually support the creatures which are at quite a low evolutionary stage. The creatures which must be supported externally, which must be clad in a kind of armour, owe their protective armour to the activity of the undines. Thus it is the undines which impart to these somewhat higher animals, in a primitive way, what we have in the cranial part of the skull. They make them, as it were, into heads.

All the beings that are invisibly present behind the visible world have their vital task in the great scheme of things. You will always notice that materialistic science breaks down when one tries to use it to explain something of the kind I have just described. It cannot be used, for instance, to explain how the lower creatures, which are scarcely any more solid than the element in which they live, manage to propel themselves forward in it, because the scientists do not know about the spiritual support provided by the gnomes. Equally, the development of an external shell will always present a problem to purely materialistic scientists, because they do not know that the undines, in their sensitivity to, and avoidance of, their own tendency to become lower animals, cast off what then appears on the somewhat higher animals as scales or some other kind of outer shell.

Again, in the case of these elemental beings, it is only our body which hinders the ordinary consciousness of today from seeing them just as it sees the leaves of plants, for example, or the somewhat higher animals.

When, however, man falls into a state of deep, dreamless sleep, and yet his sleep is not dreamless, because through the gift of Inspiration it has become transparent, then his spiritual gaze perceives the undines rising up out of that astral sea in which, on falling asleep, he was engulfed, submerged by the gnomes. In deep sleep the undines become visible. Sleep extinguishes ordinary consciousness, but the sleep which is illumined by clear consciousness is filled with the wonderful world of ever-changing fluidity, a fluidity that rises up in all kinds of ways to create the metamorphoses of the undines. Just as our day consciousness perceives creatures around us that have firm contours, a clear night consciousness would present to us these ever changing beings, which themselves rise up and sink down again like the waves of the sea. All deep sleep is filled with a moving sea of living beings, a moving sea of undines all around the human being.

It is different in the case of the sylphs. In a way they also complement the being of certain animals, but now in the other direction. The gnomes and undines add what is of the nature of the head to the animals where this is lacking. Birds, however, as I described to you, are actually pure head; they are entirely head organization. The sylphs add to the birds in a spiritual way what they lack as the physical complement of their head organization. They complement the bird kingdom with what corresponds to the metabolism and limbs in man. If the birds fly about in the air with atrophied legs, so much the more powerfully developed is the limb system of the sylphs. They may be said to represent in the air, in a spiritual way, what the cow represents below in physical matter. This is why I was able to say yesterday that it is in connection with the birds that the sylphs have their ego, have what connects them with the earth. Man acquires his ego on the earth. What connects the sylphs with the earth is the bird kingdom. The sylphs are indebted to the bird kingdom for their ego, or at least for the consciousness of their ego.

Now when someone has slept through the night, has had around him the astral sea that gives rise to the most manifold undine forms, and then perceives a dream on awakening, if this dream he wakes up to were not masked in things reminiscent of life or symbolic representations of the organs, if he were to see the unmasked dream, he would be confronted by the world of the sylphs. But these sylphs would assume for him a strange form; they would appear much as the sun might if it wished to send to human beings something which would affect them strangely, something which would have a soporific spiritual effect on their sleep. We shall hear in a moment why this is so. If someone were to perceive his unmasked dream on awakening, he would see light fluttering towards him, the essence of light fluttering towards him. He would find this an unpleasant experience, particularly also because the limbs of these sylphs would, as it were, spin and weave around him. He would feel as though the light were attacking him from all sides, as if the light were something that beset him and to which he was extraordinarily sensitive. Now and then he would perhaps also feel this to be like a caress from the light. What I really wish to indicate here is only that the light, with its upholding, gently touching quality, actually approaches in the sylph's form.

When we come to the fire spirits, we find that they complement the fleeting nature of the butterflies. A butterfly itself develops as little as possible of its actual physical body; it leaves this as tenuous as possible. It is a creature of light. The fire spirits appear as beings which complement the butterfly's body, so that we can get the following impression. If, on the one hand, we had a physical butterfly before us, and pictured it suitably enlarged, and on the other hand a fire spirit—they are, it is true, rarely together, except in the circumstances which I mentioned to you yesterday—then, if these two were welded together, we would get something resembling a winged human being, actually a winged human being. We need only increase the size of the butterfly, and adapt the size of the fire spirit to human proportions, and from this we would get something like a winged human being.

This again shows that the fire spirits are in fact the

complement to creatures nearest to what is spiritual; they complement them, so to say, in a downward direction. Gnomes and undines complement in an upward direction, towards the head; sylphs and fire spirits complement the birds and butterflies in a downward direction. Thus the fire spirits must be seen in connection with the butterflies.

Now in the same way that man can, as it were, penetrate the dreams of sleep, so he can also penetrate waking day life. But here he makes use of his physical body in quite a robust way. This, too, I have described in essays in the *Goetheanum*.* When he does this, man is totally unable to realize that he would, if he could, actually always see the fire spirits in his waking life, for the fire spirits are inwardly related to his thoughts, to everything which proceeds from the organization of the head. But when someone has progressed so far that he can remain completely in waking consciousness, but nevertheless stand in a certain sense outside himself, viewing himself from outside as a thinking being, while standing firmly on the earth, then he will become aware how the fire spirits are the element in the world which makes our thoughts perceptible from the other side.

Thus the perceiving of the fire spirits can enable man to *see* himself as thinker, not merely to *be* the thinker—and, as such, hatch out thoughts—but actually to behold how the thoughts run their course. In that case, however, thoughts cease to be bound to the human being; they reveal themselves to be world thoughts; they are active and move as impulses in the world. Then one finds that the human head only calls forth the illusion that thoughts are enclosed inside the skull. They are only reflected there; their mirrored images are there. What underlies these thoughts belongs to the sphere of the fire spirits. On entering this sphere one sees thoughts to be not only what they are in themselves, but the thought content of

---

* See *On the Life of the Soul* (op. cit.).

the world, which, at the same time, is actually rich in imaginative content. The power to stand outside oneself is the power that enables one to arrive at the realization that thoughts are world thoughts.

I venture to add: when we behold what is to be seen upon the earth, not from a human body, but from the sphere of the fire spirits—that is, from the Saturn nature that projects into the earth, as it were—then we gain exactly the picture of the evolution of the Earth which I have described in *Occult Science—an Outline*. This book is actually so composed that the thoughts appear as the thought content of the world, seen from the perspective of the fire spirits.

You see, these things do have a deep and real significance. But they also have a deep and real significance for man in other ways. Take the gnomes and undines: they exist in the world, one can say, which borders on human consciousness; they are already beyond the threshold. Ordinary consciousness is protected from seeing these beings, for the fact is that these beings are not all benevolent. The benevolent beings are, for instance, those which I described yesterday as working in the most varied ways on plant growth. But not all these beings are well-disposed. And the moment one breaks through into the world where they are active, one finds there not only the well-disposed beings but the malevolent ones as well. One must first form a conception about which of them are well-disposed and which of them malevolent. This is not so easy, as you will see from the way I must describe the malevolent ones. The main difference between the ill-disposed beings and the well-disposed is that the latter are always drawn more to the plant and mineral kingdoms, whereas the ill-disposed are drawn to the animal and human kingdoms. Some, which are even more malevolent, try to approach the kingdoms of the plants and the minerals as well. But one can gain quite a fair idea of the malevolence, which the beings of this realm can have, when one turns to those which are drawn to human beings and animals, who in particular try to accomplish in man what the higher hierarchies entrust to the well-disposed beings for the plant and mineral world.

You see, there exist ill-disposed beings from the realm of the gnomes and undines, which approach human beings and animals, and cause the complement with which they are supposed to endow only the lower animals to come to physical realization in human beings. This element is already present in man, but their aim is that it should be manifested physically in human beings—and also in animals. Through the presence of these malevolent gnome and undine beings, animal and plant life of a low order—parasites—live in human beings and in animals. These malevolent beings are the begetters of parasites. The moment man crosses the threshold of the spiritual world, he at once meets the trickery that exists in this world. Snares are everywhere, and he must first learn something from the goblins—namely, to be attentive. This is something that spiritualists, for example, can never manage! Everywhere there are snares. Now someone might say: Why then are these malevolent gnome and undine beings there, if they engender parasites? Well, if they were not there, man would never be able to develop within himself the power to evolve brain substance. And here we meet something of extraordinary significance.

If you think of the human being as consisting of metabolism and limbs, of the chest—that is, the rhythmical system—and then the head—that is, the system of nerves and senses—there are certain things about which you must be quite clear. Down below processes are taking place—let us leave out the rhythmical sphere—and above processes are taking place. If you look at the processes taking place below as a whole, you find that in ordinary life they have one result that is usually disregarded. These processes are those of elimination: through the intestines, through the kidneys, and so on; and all of them have their outlet in a downward direction. They are mostly regarded simply as processes of elimination. But this is non-sense. Elimination does not take place merely in order to eliminate, but to the same degree in which the products of elimination arise something arises spiritually in the lower sphere of man which resembles what the brain is, physically, above. What occurs in the lower man is a process arrested halfway as far as its physical development is concerned. Elimination takes place because the process passes over into the spiritual. In man's upper sphere the process is taken to its conclusion. What below is only spiritual there assumes physical form. Above we have the physical brain, below a spiritual brain. And if what is eliminated below were to be subjected to a further process, if one were to continue the transformation, then ultimately such metamorphosis would give rise to the human brain.

The human brain is the further evolved product of elim-ination. This is something which is of immense importance, in regard to medicine for instance, and it is something of which doctors in the sixteenth and seventeenth centuries were still fully aware. Of course today people speak in a very derogatory manner—and rightly in many respects—of the 'quacks of old who dealt in filth'. But this is because they do not know that such filth still contained 'mummies' of the spirit. Naturally this is not intended as a glorification of what has figured as quackery in past centuries, but I am referring to the many truths with connections as deep as those I have just cited.

The brain is a higher metamorphosis of the products of elimination. Hence the connection between diseases of the brain and intestinal diseases, and also their cure.

You see, because gnomes and undines exist, because there is a world in which they are able to live, the forces exist that are certainly capable of giving rise to parasites in man's lower sphere; but at the same time, in man's upper sphere, this gives rise to metamorphosis into the brain of the products of elimination. It would be absolutely impossible for us to have a brain if the world were not so ordered that gnomes and undines can exist.

What holds good for gnomes and undines in regard to destructive powers—for destruction and disintegration also proceed from the brain—holds goods for sylphs and fire spirits in regard to regenerative powers. Here again the well-disposed sylphs and fire spirits keep away from human beings and animals, and busy themselves with plant growth in the way I have indicated; but there are also those which are malevolent. These ill-disposed beings are above all concerned in carrying what should only have its place up above in the regions of air and warmth down into the watery and earthy regions.

Now if you wish to study what happens when these sylph beings carry what belongs up above down into the watery and earthy regions, look at the deadly nightshade (*Atropa bella-donna*). The flower of this plant, if I may put it so, has been kissed by the sylph, and what could be beneficent juices have been changed into poisonous ones.

Here you have what may be called a displacement of spheres. It is right when the sylphs develop their enveloping forces up above, as I have already described, where the light literally comes and touches you all over—for the bird world needs this. But if the sylph descends, and makes use in the plant world below of what it should employ up above, a potent vegetable poison is engendered. Parasitic beings arise through gnomes and undines; and through sylphs arise the poisons which are in fact a heavenly element that has streamed down too far, has descended to earth. When people or certain animals eat the fruit of the deadly nightshade, which looks like a cherry, except that it conceals itself in the calyx (it is pushed down—you can see what I have just described when you look at the plant)—when people or certain animals eat the berry, it is fatal to them. But just look at the thrushes and blackbirds;

they perch on the plant and get from it the best food in the world. What is present in the belladonna belongs rightly to the sphere they inhabit.

It is a remarkable thing that animals and human beings whose lower organs are earthbound should experience as poison what has become corrupted on the earth in the deadly nightshade, yet birds such as thrushes and blackbirds, which should really get this in a spiritual way from the sylphs—and indeed through the benevolent sylphs do so obtain it—are able to assimilate something that has been thrust down to the earth from their region above They find nourishment in what is poison for beings more bound to the earth.

Thus you get a conception of how gnomes and undines impel what is of a parasitic nature to strive upwards from the earth towards other beings, while poisons on the other hand filter downwards from above.

And when the fire spirits imbue themselves with the impulses that belong in the region of the butterflies, and are of great use to them in their development—when the fire spirits carry those impulses down into the fruits, we get the poisonous almonds that are found in some species of almond. The poison is carried into the fruit of the almond trees through the activity of the fire spirits. And yet the fruit of the almond could not come into existence at all if those same fire spirits did not in a beneficial way burn, as it were, what is the edible part in other fruits. Only look at the almond. With other fruits you have the white kernel at the centre and around it the flesh of the fruit. With the almond you have the kernel there in the centre, and around it the flesh of the fruit is quite burnt up. That is the activity of the fire spirits. And if this activity miscarries, if what the fire spirits are bringing about is not confined to the brown shell, where their activity can still be beneficial, and something of what should be engaged in developing the shell penetrates into the white kernel, then the almond becomes poisonous.

And so you have gained a picture of the beings lying immediately beyond the threshold of normal awareness, and of how, if they follow their impulses, they become the bearers of parasitic and poisonous principles, and therewith of illnesses. Now it becomes clear how, when healthy, we raise ourselves above the forces that take hold of us in illness. For illness springs from the malevolence of the beings necessary for the regeneration of the world of nature, for its shooting and sprouting growth, but also for its fading and decay.

These are the things which, arising from instinctive clairvoyance, underlie such intuitions as those of the Indian Brahma, Vishnu and Shiva. Brahma represented the being at work in the cosmic sphere, which may legitimately approach man. Vishnu represented the cosmic sphere which may only approach man in so far as what has been built up must again be broken down, in so far as it must be continually transformed. Shiva represented everything connected with the forces of destruction. And in the ancient times of the flowering of Indian civilization it was said: 'Brahma is intimately related to all that is of the nature of the fire spirits and the sylphs; Vishnu with all that is of the nature of sylphs and undines; Shiva with all that is of the nature of undines and gnomes.' Generally speaking, when we go back to these more ancient conceptions, we find everywhere the pictorial expressions for what must be sought today as immanent in the secrets of nature.

Yesterday we studied the connection of these invisible folk with the plant world; today we have added their connection with the world of the animals. Everywhere beings on this side of the threshold interact with those from beyond it; and vice versa. Only when one knows the living interaction of both these kinds of beings does one really understand how the visible world unfolds. Knowledge of the supersensible world is indeed very, very necessary for man, for the moment he passes through the gate of death he no longer has the sense-perceptible world around him, but initially this other world begins to be his world. At his present stage of evolution man cannot find correct access to the other world unless he has recognized in physical manifestations the written characters which point to this other world; if he has not learned to read in the creatures of the earth, in the creatures of the water, in the creatures of the air and in what I'd like to call the creatures of the light, the butterflies, the signs of elemental beings which are our companions between death and a new birth. What we see of the creatures here between birth and death is, so to speak, their crude, dense part. We only learn to recognize what belongs to them as their supersensible nature when, with insight and understanding, we enter into this supersensible world.

Lecture 9

4 November 1923

We come to know the beings of the sense world by observing the way they live and act, and it is the same with the beings about which I have been speaking and shall continue to speak in these lectures, the elemental beings of nature. Invisibly and supersensibly present behind what is physical and perceptible to the senses, they participate in all the happenings of the world just as, or rather in a higher sense than, do physical, sense-perceptible beings.

Now you will readily be able to imagine that to these beings the world appears somewhat different than it does to the beings of the sense world, for they do not possess a physical body as the latter do. Everything which they grasp or perceive in the world must be different from what enters the human eye, for example. This is indeed the case. The human being experiences the earth, for instance, as the cosmic body on which he moves about. He even finds it slightly inconvenient when through some atmospheric condition or other, as occasionally happens, this cosmic body becomes softened and he sinks into it, even slightly. He likes to feel the earth as something hard, as something into which he does not sink.

This whole way of experiencing things, this whole attitude towards the earth, is, however, completely alien to the gnomes; they sink down everywhere, because for them the whole earth body is primarily a hollow space through which they can pass. They can penetrate everywhere; rocks and metals present no hindrance to their way of—shall I say walking about or swimming about? There are no words in our language which really express the way the gnomes move about inside the body of the earth. It is just that they have an inner experience, an inner perception, of the different ingredients of the earth; when they wander along a vein of metal they have a different experience from when they make their way through a layer of limestone. All this, however, the gnomes feel inwardly, for through all such things they penetrate unhindered. They have not the least idea that the earth exists. Their idea is that there is a space in which they perceive certain experiences: the experience of gold, the experience of mercury, of tin, of silica, and so on. This is to express it in human language, not in the language of the gnomes. Their language is far more perceptive; and it is just because their whole life is spent in journeying along all the veins and seams—continually journeying through them—that they acquire the very pronounced intellectuality about which I have spoken to you. Through this they acquire their comprehensive knowledge, for the metals and the earth reveal everything to them of what is outside in the universe, as though in a mirror they experience everything which is outside in the universe. But for the earth itself the gnomes have no perception, only for its different ingredients, and for the different kinds of inner experience which these offer.

Because of this the gnomes have a quite particular gift for receiving the impressions which come from the moon. It is towards the moon that they continually direct their attentive listening, and in this respect they have a—I cannot say congenital (it is so difficult to find the right words)—but acquired neurasthenia (nervous debility). Of course, what for us is an illness is for these gnomes their actual life element. For them this is no illness but simply a matter of course. It is what gives them that inner receptivity towards all the things of which I have spoken. But it also gives them their inner receptivity

144 HARMONY OF THE CREATIVE WORD

towards the phenomena connected with the phases of the moon.

They follow the changes in the moon cycle with such close attention—I have already described their power of attention to you—that it actually alters their form. When, therefore, one follows the existence of a gnome, one gains a quite different impression at full moon from that gained at new moon, and again at the intermediate phases.

At full moon the gnomes are ill at ease. Physical moonlight does not suit them, and at that time they thrust the whole feeling of their existence outwards. They circumscribe themselves, as it were, with a spiritual skin. At full moon they push the feeling of their existence towards the boundary of their body. And in full moonlight, if one has imaginative perception for such things, they really appear like little shining, mail-clad knights. They are clad in a kind of spiritual armour, and this it is which pushes outwards in their skin to arm them against the moonlight which makes them feel so uncomfortable. But when the time of new moon approaches the gnomes become positively transparent, wonderful to see, inwardly irradiated with a glittering play of colours. One sees within them, as it were, the processes of a whole world. It is as though one were to look into the human brain, not as an anatomist investigating cell tissues, but as one who perceives inside the brain the shimmering and sparkling of thoughts. That is how these transparent little folk, the gnomes, appear to one, as though the play of thoughts is revealed within them. It is just at new moon that the gnomes are so particularly interesting, for each of them bears a whole world within himself; and one can say that within this world there actually lies the mystery of the moon.

If one unveils this moon mystery, one comes upon truly remarkable discoveries, for one reaches the conclusion that at the present time the moon is continually coming closer— naturally you must not take this in a crude way, as though the moon were moving towards the earth at a fast pace—but each year it does in fact come somewhat nearer. Each year the moon is actually slightly nearer to the earth. One recognizes this from the ever more vigorous play of the moon's forces in the world of the gnomes during the time of the new moon. And to this coming nearer of the moon the attentiveness of these goblins is quite specially directed; for in producing results from the way in which the moon affects them they see their chief mission in the universe. They await with intense expectation the time when the moon will again unite with the earth; and they assemble all their forces in order to be armed in readiness for this time, when the moon re-unites with the earth, for they will then use the moon substance gradually to disperse the outer substance of the earth into the universe. The substance must pass away.

Because they hold this task in view these goblins or gnomes feel themselves to be of quite special importance, for they gather together the most varied experiences from the whole of earth existence, and they hold themselves in readiness, when all earthly substance will have been dispersed into the universe—after the transition to Jupiter evolution—to preserve what is good in the earth structure in order to incorporate this in Jupiter, as a kind of bony skeleton.

You see, when one looks at this process from the aspect of the gnomes, one gains a first stimulus, a first capacity, to picture how our earth would appear if all the water were taken away from it. Just consider how, in the western hemisphere, everything is orientated from north to south, and how, in the eastern hemisphere, everything is orientated from east to west. Thus, if you were to do away with all the water, America, with its mountains and what lies under the sea, would appear as something which proceeds from north to south; and looking towards Europe you would find that, in the eastern hemisphere, corresponding to the chain of the Alps, the Carpathians and so on, the orientation is in an east-west

direction. You would get something like the structure of the cross in the earth.

When one gains insight into this, one gains the impression that this is really the united gnome world of old Moon. The ancestors of our earth gnomes, the Moon gnomes, gathered together their Moon experiences and from them fashioned this structure, this firm structure of the solid fabric of the earth, so that the solid structure of the earth actually arose from the experiences of the gnomes of old Moon.

These are the things which reveal themselves in relation to the gnome world. Through them the gnomes acquire an interesting, an extraordinarily interesting relationship to the whole evolution of the universe. They always carry over the solid element from one stage to the next. They are the pre-servers in evolution of the continuity of the solid structure, and thus they preserve the solid structure from one cosmic body to another. It is one of the most interesting studies to examine these supersensible, spiritual beings and to observe their special task, for this gives one a first impression of how every kind of being existing in the world shares in the task of working on the whole form and structure of the world.

Now let us pass over from the gnomes to the undines, the water beings. Here a very remarkable idea presents itself. These beings do not have the need for life that human beings or animals have, nor the need for life that the animals have, however instinctively, but one could almost say that the undines, and also the sylphs, have a need for death instead. In a cosmic way they are really like the gnat which casts itself into the flame. They only feel themselves to be truly alive when they die. This is extraordinarily interesting. Here on the physical earth everything desires to live, for all that has vitality is prized, all that sprouts and shoots with life. But once we have crossed the threshold, all these beings say to us that it is death which is really the true beginning of life. This can be felt by these beings. Let us take the undines. You know, perhaps, that sailors who travel a great deal on the sea find that in July, August and September in the Baltic—further to the west this is already the case in June—the sea makes a peculiar impression, and they say that it is beginning to blossom. It begins to sprout, as it were; but it begins to sprout out of everything that is decaying in the sea. The process of decay in the sea makes itself felt: it imparts to the sea a peculiar putrescent smell.

All this, however, is different for the undines. It causes them no unpleasant sensations; but when the millions and millions of water creatures which perish in the sea start decomposing, the sea becomes for the undines the most wonderful phosphorescent play of colours. It shines and glitters with every possible colour. Especially does the sea glitter for them, inwardly and outwardly, in every shade of blue, violet and green. The whole process of decomposition in the sea becomes a glimmering and gleaming of darker colours up to green. But these colours are realities for the undines, and one can see how, in this play of colours in the sea, they absorb the colours into themselves. They draw these colours into their own bodily nature. They become like them, they themselves become phosphorescent. And as they absorb the play of colours, as they themselves become phosphorescent, there arises in the undines something like a longing, an immense longing to rise upwards, to soar upwards. Upwards they soar, led by this longing, and with this longing they offer themselves to the beings of the higher hierarchies—to the angels, archangels and so on—as earthly sustenance; and in this sacrifice they find their bliss. They then live on within the higher hierarchies.

And thus we see the remarkable fact that each year, with the return of early spring, these beings evolve upwards from unfathomable depths. There they take part in the life of the earth by working on the plant kingdom in the way I have described. Then however they pour themselves, as it were, into the water, and take up by means of their own bodily nature the phosphorescence of the water, the decaying matter, and bear it upwards with an intensity of longing. Then in a vast, in a magnificent cosmic picture, one sees how, emanating from earthly water, the colours carried upwards by the undines, and which have spiritual substantiality, provide the higher hierarchies with their sustenance—how the earth becomes the source of nourishment in that the very essence of the undines' longing is to let themselves be consumed by higher beings. There they live on; there they enter into their eternity. Thus every year there is a continual upstreaming of these undines, whose inner nature is formed out of the earthly sphere, and who radiate upwards, filled with the longing to offer themselves as nourishment to higher beings.

And now let us proceed to the sylphs. In the course of the year birds die. I described to you how these dying birds possess spiritualized substance, and how they desire to give this spiritualized substance over to higher worlds in order to release it from the earth. But here an intermediary is needed. And these intermediaries are the sylphs. It is a fact that dying birds continually fill the air with astrality. This astrality is of a

lower order, but it is nevertheless astrality; it is astral substance. In this astrality flutter—or hover might be a better
word—in this astrality hover the sylphs. They take up what
comes from the world of dying birds and carry it, again with a
feeling of longing, up into the heights, only desiring to be
breathed by the beings of the higher hierarchies. They offer
themselves as that which supplies a breathing element to the
higher hierarchies. Again a magnificent spectacle. With the
realm of dying birds this astral, inwardly radiant substance is
seen to pass over into the air. The sylphs flash like blue
lightning through the air, and into their blue lightning, which
assumes first greener, then redder hues, they absorb the
astrality which comes from the bird world, and dart upwards
like upward flashing lightning. And if one follows this beyond
the boundaries of space, it becomes what is breathed by
beings of the higher hierarchies.

Thus one can say that the gnomes carry one world over into
another as far as its structure is concerned. They go with
evolution in a horizontal direction, as it were—this is merely
an analogy. The other beings—the undines, the sylphs—carry
upwards what they experience as bliss in yielding themselves
up to death, in being consumed, in being breathed. There
they continue to live within the higher hierarchies, experiencing their eternity within them.

And when we go on to the fire spirits, only think how the
dust on the butterfly's wings seems to dissolve into nothing
with the death of the butterfly. But it does not really dissolve
into nothing. What is shed as dust from the butterfly's wings is
the most highly spiritualized matter. And all this passes like
microscopic comets into the heat ether which surrounds the
earth, each single particle of dust passes like a microscopic
comet into the heat ether of the earth. When in the course of
the year the butterfly world approaches its end, all this
becomes glittering and shimmering, an inner glittering and
shimmering. And into this glittering and shimmering the fire

spirits pour themselves; they absorb it. There it continues to glitter and shimmer, and they, too, get a feeling of longing. They bear what they have thus absorbed up into the heights. And now one sees—I have already described this to you from another aspect—how the glittering and shimmering carried outwards from the butterfly's wings by the fire spirits shines forth into world space. But it does not only shine forth; it streams forth. And it is this which provides the particular view of the earth which the higher hierarchies perceive. The beings of the higher hierarchies gaze upon the earth, and what they principally see is this butterfly and insect existence which has been carried outwards by the fire spirits; and the fire spirits find their highest ecstasy in the realization that it is they who present themselves before the spiritual eyes of the higher hierarchies. They find their highest ecstasy in being beheld by the gaze, by the spiritual eyes, of the higher hierarchies, in being absorbed into them. They strive upwards towards these beings and carry to them knowledge of the earth.

Thus we see how these elemental beings are the intermediaries between the earth and the spirit-cosmos. We see the drama of the phosphorescent upsurge of the undines, which pass away in the sea of light and flame of the higher hierarchies as their sustenance; we see the upward flashing greenish-reddish lightning, which is breathed where the earth continually passes over into eternity, the eternal survival of the fire spirits, whose activity never ceases. For whereas, here on earth, birds tend to die at a particular time of year, the fire spirits make sure that what is to be seen of them pours out into the universe throughout the entire year. Thus the earth is as though cloaked in a mantle of fire. Seen from outside the earth appears fiery. But everything is brought about by beings who see the things of the earth quite differently from how man sees them. As already mentioned, man's experience of the earth is of a hard substance on which he stands and walks about. For the gnomes it is a transparent globe, a hollow body. For the undines water is something in which they perceive the phosphorizing process, which they can take into themselves as living experience. Sylphs see in the astrality of the air, which emanates from dying birds, something that makes them into more actively flashing lightning than they would otherwise be, for in itself the lightning of these sylphs is dull and bluish. And then again the disintegration of butterfly existence is something which continually envelops the earth as though with a shell of fire. Beholding this, it seems as though the earth were surrounded by a wonderful fiery painting; and there to one side, when one looks upwards from the earth, one beholds these lightning flashes, these phosphorescent and evanescent undines. All this shows us that here on earth the elemental nature spirits move and work actively, striving upwards and passing away in the fiery mantle of the earth. In reality, however, they do not pass away, but they find their eternal existence by passing over into beings of the higher hierarchies.

All this, however, which ultimately appears like a wonderful painting of the world, is the expression of what happens on earth, for to begin with and in its initial stages it all takes place on the earth. We human beings are always present in what is there taking place; and the fact is—even if in his ordinary consciousness man is at first incapable of grasping what surrounds him—that every night we are involved in the movement and activity of these beings, that we ourselves take part as ego and as astral body in what these beings carry out.

But it is the gnomes especially which really find it quite entertaining to observe a person asleep—not the physical body in bed, but the person's astral body and ego outside his physical body, for what the gnomes see is someone who thinks in the spirit but does not know it. He does not know that his thoughts live in the spiritual. And again for the undines it is inexplicable that man knows himself so little; the same is true for the sylphs, and likewise for the fire spirits.

On the physical plane, you see, it is certainly often unpleasant to have gnats and the like fluttering around one at night. But the spiritual man, the ego and astral body—at night these are surrounded by the life and activity of elemental beings; and being thus surrounded by life and activity is a constant admonition to man to advance in his consciousness in order to know more about the world.

Now, therefore, I can try to give you an idea of how these beings—gnomes, undines, sylphs and fire spirits—flit about, of what happens when we begin to hear what amuses them in us, and of what they would have us do when they admonish us to advance in consciousness. Yes, you see, here come the gnomes and speak somewhat as follows:

> You dream yourself,
> And shun awakening.

The gnomes know that man possesses his ego as though in a dream, that he must first awaken in order to arrive at his true ego. They see this quite clearly, and call to him in his sleep:

> You dream yourself

—they mean during the day—

> And shun awakening.

Then there sounds forth from the undines:

> You think the deeds of angels . . .

Man does not know that his thoughts are really with the angels:

> You think the deeds of angels
> And know it not.

And from the sylphs there sounds to sleeping man:

Creative might shines to you,
You divine it not.
You feel its strength

—the strength of creative might—

And live it not.

Such approximately are the words of the sylphs, the words of the undines, the words of the gnomes.

The words of the fire spirits:

Divine will offers you strength,
You accept it not.
With its strength you will,

—with the strength of divine will—

Yet thrust it from you.

All this is the admonition to progress in consciousness. These beings, which do not enter into physical existence, wish man to make a move onwards with his consciousness, so that he may be able to participate in their world.

And when one has thus entered into what these beings have to say to man, one also gradually understands how they give expression to their own nature, somewhat in this way:

The gnomes:

I maintain the power of root nature,
It creates for me the body of forms.

The undines:

I bestir the water's power of growth,
It creates for me substance of life.

The sylphs:

> I quaff the airy force of life,
> It fills me with the power of existence.

And the fire spirits—it is very difficult to find any kind of earthly words for what they do, because their sphere is far removed from earthly life and earthly activity.

Fire spirits:

> I consume* the striving power of fire,
> Into spirituality of soul it releases me.

You see, I have endeavoured to the best of my ability to give you an idea of how these beings of the elemental kingdom characterize themselves; and of the admonitions which they initially impart to man. But they are not so unfriendly to man as only to suggest to him what is negative by nature, but pithy and positive sayings also proceed from them. And we experience these sayings as being of immense, of gigantic significance. In such matters as these you must acquire a sense for whether a saying is uttered merely in human words, however beautiful they may be, or whether it sounds forth as though cosmically from the whole mighty army of the gnomes. What is important, what makes the difference, is the way such words arise, where they really come from. And when man hearkens to the gnomes, after they have uttered the admonitions which I have written on the board, then there sounds towards him from the massed chorus of the gnomes:

Strive to awaken!

Here the significance is the mighty moral impression created by such words when they stream through the universe, arising from the massed chorus of infinitely many single voices.

---

* Here Rudolf Steiner coined a word from *verdauen*, to digest: *däuen—ich däue*, to express, not ordinary digestion, but a fiery consuming process.

And from the undine chorus resounds:

Think in the spirit!

With the chorus of sylphs things are not so simple. When the gnomes appear like shining armoured knights in full moonlight there resounds from them as though from the earth's depths: 'Strive to awaken.' When the undines soar upwards filled with the longing to be consumed, then in this upsoaring there sounds back to the earth: 'Think in the Spirit.' But from the sylphs, in the heights as they allow themselves to be inhaled up above, and seem to disappear in bluish-reddish-greenish lightning into cosmic light, flash into the light and disappear in it, there sounds down:

Live and create breathing existence!

And the words of the fire spirits resound as, in fiery anger—an anger which is not felt to be annihilating, but rather as something which man must receive from the cosmos—as in fiery but at the same time enthusiastic anger, they carry what is theirs into the fiery mantle of the earth. Here the sound is not like that of single voices massed together, but from the whole circumference there resounds as with a mighty voice of thunder:

Receive in love the will-power of the gods!

Naturally, one can turn one's attention away from all this, and then one does not perceive it. Whether or not man does perceive such things depends upon his own free choice. But when man does perceive them he knows that they are an integral part of cosmic existence, that something actually occurs when gnomes, undines, sylphs and fire spirits manifest in the way described. And the gnomes are not only present for man in the way I have already portrayed, but they are there to let their world words sound forth from the earth, the undines to let their world words soar upwards, the sylphs theirs downwards from above, the fire spirits theirs like a chorus, like the massing of a mighty uplifting of voices.

Yes, this is how it could sound when transposed into words. But these words belong to the World Word, and even though we do not hear them with ordinary consciousness these words are not without significance for mankind. For the primeval idea, which had its source in instinctive clairvoyance, that the world was born out of the Word is indeed a profound truth, but the World Word is not some collection of syllables gathered from just a few sources; the World Word sounds forth from a countless multitude of beings. Countless, countless beings have something to say in the totality of the world, and the World Word sounds forth from the concordance of these countless beings. The general abstract truth that the world is born out of the Word cannot bring this home to us in its fullness. One thing alone can do this, namely, that we gradually arrive at a concrete understanding of how the World Word in all its different nuances is composed of the voices of individual beings, so that these different nuances contribute their sound, their utterance, to the great world harmony, the mighty world melody, in the Word's act of creation.

When the gnome chorus sounds forth its 'Strive to awaken' this—translated into gnome language—is the force which is active in bringing about the human skeletal system, and the system of movement in general.

When the undines utter 'Think in the spirit', they utter—translated into Undine—what pours itself as World Word into man in order to give form to the metabolic organs.

When the sylphs, as they are breathed, allow their 'Live and create breathing existence' to stream downwards, there penetrates into man, moving and pulsating everywhere in him, the force which endows him with the organs of the rhythmical system.

And if one attends to the fire-spirit sounds that resound and stream in from the fire mantle of the world with a voice of thunder, then one finds that this sounding manifests as image or reflection. It streams in from the fire mantle—this sounding force of the word. And the nerves and senses of every human being, every human head we might say, is a miniature image of what—translated into the language of fire spirits—rings out as: 'Receive in love the will-power of the gods'. This 'Receive in love the will-power of the gods' is what is active in the highest substances of the world. When man is going through his development in the life between death and a new birth, this transforms what he brought with him through the gate of death into what will later be the human organs of the nerves and senses. So we have:

	System of movement
Chorus of gnomes:	Strive to awaken.
	Metabolic organization
Undines:	Think in the spirit.
	Rhythmical system
Sylphs:	Live and create breathing existence.
	System of nerves and senses
Fire spirits:	Receive in love the will-power of the gods.

Thus you see that what lies beyond the threshold is part of our own nature, you see how it takes us into the active divine forces, into what lives and works in all forms of existence. And when one calls to mind what an earlier epoch divined, and is expressed in the words:

Grant me a vision of Nature's forces,
That bind the world, all its seeds and sources

> And innermost life—all this I shall see,
> And stop peddling in words that mean nothing to me . . .*

—one is impelled to say that this must come to realization in the further course of mankind's development. We rummage and peddle in words, with all our knowledge, if we have no insight into the germinal powers, the vital seed forces, that build up the human being in the most varied ways.

We can therefore say that the system of movement, the metabolic system, the rhythmical system, the system of nerves and senses are one whole that comes together as there sounds upwards from below: 'Strive to awaken'; 'Think in the Spirit'—and from above downwards, mingling with the upward-striving words, 'Live and create breathing existence'; 'Receive in love the will-power of the gods'.

This 'Receive in love the will-power of the gods' is the calm creative element in the head. What strives from below upwards in 'Think in the Spirit', from above downwards in 'Live and create breathing existence', specifically lives and works together in such a way that it creates an image of itself in the way in which human breathing passes over in a rhythmical way into the activity of the blood. And what implants into us the instruments of the senses, this is what streams from above downwards in 'Receive in love the will-power of the gods'. But what works in our walking, in our standing, in our moving of the arms and hands, everything in fact which brings man into the manifestation of his element of will, this sounds forth in 'Strive to awaken'.

Thus you see how man is a symphony of that World Word which can be interpreted at its lowest level in the way I have presented it to you. Then this World Word ascends to the higher hierarchies, whose task it is to unfold even more than

---

* Goethe, *Faust* Part 1, Scene 1. Tr. by David Luke. Oxford University Press 1987.

the World Word in order that the cosmos may arise and evolve. But what these elemental beings have, as it were, summoned into the world is the final reverberation of that creative, upbuilding, form-giving World Word which underlies all activity and all existence.

Gnomes	You dream yourself, And shun awakening. I maintain the power of root nature, It creates for me the body of forms.
Undines	You think the deeds of angels And know it not. I bestir the water's power of growth, It forms for me substance of life.
Sylphs	Creative might shines to you, You divine it not; You feel its strength And live it not. I quaff the airy force of life, It fills me with the power of being.
Fire spirits	Divine will offers you strength, You accept it not. With its strength you will, Yet thrust it from you. I consume the striving power of fire, Into soul-spirit it releases me.
Chorus of gnomes	Strive to awaken!
Undines	Think in the spirit!
Sylphs	Live and create breathing existence!
Fire spirits	Receive in love the will-power of the gods!

Gnomen	Du träumst dich selbst,
	Und meidest das Erwachen.
	Ich halte die Wurzelwesenskraft,
	Sie schaffet mir den Formenleib.
Undinen	Du denkst die Engelwerke,
	Und weisst es nicht.
	Ich bewege die Wasserwachstumskraft,
	Sie bildet mir den Lebensstoff.
Sylphen	Dir leuchtet die Schöpfermacht,
	Du ahnst es nicht;
	Du fühlest ihre Kraft,
	Und lebst sie nicht.
	Ich schlürfe die luft'ge Lebekraft,
	Sie füllet mich mit Seinsgewalt.
Feuerwesen	Dir kraftet Götterwille,
	Du empfängst ihn nicht.
	Du willst mit seiner Kraft
	Und stossest ihn von dir.
	Ich däue die Feuerstrebekraft,
	Sie erlöst mich in Seelengeistigkeit.
Gnomenchor	Erstrebe zu erwachen!
Undinen	Denke im Geiste!
Sylphen	Lebe schaffend atmendes Dasein!
Feuerwesen	Empfange liebend Götterwillenskraft!

Part Four

The Secrets of the Human Organism

'Physical natural laws, etheric natural laws, are the characters of a script which depicts the spiritual world. We only understand these things when we are able to conceive them as written characters from spiritual worlds.'

Lecture 10

9 November 1923

In these lectures I have given recently you will have seen that everything was directed towards an integrated view of world phenomena such as might ultimately give rise to a really comprehensive study of man. Everything we have been studying here was intended to increase our knowledge of man. Such a knowledge of man will only become possible when it begins with the lowest forms of the world of phenomena, everything that the world of physical substance reveals to us. What has begun like this, with the study of the world of physical substance, must end with the study of the world of the hierarchies. It is in proceeding from the lowest forms of physical substance up to the highest forms of spiritual existence that we must seek to discover what will eventually lead to a true knowledge of man. For the present these lectures will offer a kind of outline sketch of such a knowledge of man.

We must be quite clear about the fact that what we now recognize as man is a product of that long cosmic evolution which I have always summarily called the Saturn, Sun, Moon, and Earth evolution. Earth evolution is not yet complete. But let us be clear about what man owes to this Earth evolution *per se*, that is to the evolutionary phase which follows the evolution of old Moon.

You see, when you move your arms and stretch them out, when you move your fingers, when you carry out any kind of external movement, everything in your organism which enables you to move your arms and legs, your head, your lips, and so on—and the forces on which man's external movements depend extend to the inmost parts of the human organism—all this was vouchsafed to man by our current planetary stage of Earth evolution. If, on the other hand, you look into everything connected with the development of the metabolism, which is enclosed by man's skin, if you look at all the metabolic functions in the physical body, you have a picture of what man owes to Moon evolution. And you have a picture of what man owes to old Sun evolution when you look into everything in him that involves some kind of rhythmical process. Breathing and blood circulation are of course the most important of these rhythmical processes, and these man owes to old Sun evolution. Everything in man comprising the system of nerves and senses, which is distributed over the whole body in people today, we owe to old Saturn evolution.

In regard to all this, however, you must bear in mind that the human being is a whole and that world evolution is a whole. When we examine old Saturn evolution in the way I did in my *Occult Science*, we mean the period of evolution that aeons and aeons ago preceded Sun, Moon and Earth evolution. But this is only one Saturn evolution, the one that eventually gave rise to the earth. Whilst the earth is evolving, another Saturn evolution also takes place. This new Saturn evolution is contained within Earth evolution; it is, so to speak, the most recent Saturn evolution. The original one that led to Earth evolution is the oldest. The Saturn evolution which was part of the old Sun is more recent, and the one that was part of the Moon still more recent. And the Saturn that today imbues the earth and is above all responsible for certain aspects of its warmth organization, this Saturn is the most recent of all. We, with our human nature, are part of this Saturn evolution.

Thus we stand within cosmic evolution. But we also stand within what surrounds us on earth. Take, for example, the mineral kingdom. We live in a state of interaction with the mineral kingdom. We take the mineral element into ourselves with our food. We also absorb it in other ways, through our breathing, and so on. We assimilate the mineral element.

But all evolution, all world processes, are different within man from what they are outside him. I have already mentioned that it is a real absurdity when people today study chemical processes in laboratories and then think that when a person eats certain foods these processes will simply continue inside him. Man is not some kind of confluence of chemical actions; inside him everything is altered. And from a certain standpoint this alteration appears in the following way.

Let us suppose that we take into ourselves something of a mineral nature. Every such mineral substance must be so far worked on within the human being that the following result is brought about. You know that we have our own individual temperature; in the healthy person this is about 37°C (98°F). In the temperature of our blood we have something that exceeds the temperature outside us. Everything which we take in as mineral substance must, however, be so transformed, so metamorphosed in our organism, that the average temperature difference between the blood and the world around us, the extent to which our body temperature exceeds the outside temperature, takes pleasure in absorbing the mineral element in us. If you eat a grain of common salt, this must be absorbed by your individual warmth, not by the warmth which you have in common with the outside world. Your own individual warmth must take pleasure in absorbing it. Everything mineral must be transformed into warmth ether. And the moment a person has something in his organism that prevents some mineral from being changed into warmth ether, at that moment he is ill.

Now let us proceed to the plant substances that man takes into himself. Man takes in plant substances; he, too, belongs to the plant kingdom inasmuch as he develops the plant element in himself. Mineral nature continually has the tendency to become warmth ether in man. The plant element continually has the tendency to become airy, to become gaseous in man. So that man has the plant element within himself as a realm of air. Everything of a plant nature that enters man, or whatever he himself develops as inner plant organization, must become airy, must be able to assume the form of air within him. If it does not assume the form of air, if his organization is such that it hinders him from letting what is of a plant nature within him pass over into the form of air, he becomes ill. Everything of animal nature that man takes in or develops within himself must—in time at least—assume a fluid, watery form. Man may not have what is of an animal nature within him, whether inwardly produced or absorbed from outside, unless at some time it submits to the process of becoming fluid. If man is not in a position to liquefy either his own or foreign animal substance so as to recreate it again in a solid state, he becomes ill. Only that in man which gives rise to the purely human form, due to man being someone who walks upright, having within him the impulses to speak and think, only that which gives man his real humanity, which raises him above the animal—and this is at most a tenth of his whole organism—may enter into the solid state and be solid form. If anything of animal or plant nature invades our solid human form, we become ill.

Everything mineral must eventually become warmth ether in man. Everything vegetable must undergo a transitional airy stage in man. Everything animal must pass through an intermediate water stage in man. Only what is human may always retain the solid earthly form within it. This is one of the secrets of the human organization.

And now, to begin with, let us leave aside everything that man has from Earth evolution *per se*—we'll be considering it all the more later on—and let us take the human metabolic system. Man has transformed it during the Earth stage, but it originally arose during old Moon evolution. We'll consider metabolism in the narrower sense of what takes place inside the human skin, including of course all eliminations. Our metabolism is subject to continual change, and this is due to the intake of food. The foods, initially outside man, enter into him and become part of the metabolic system.

The metabolic system converts what belonged to man's surroundings into what is essentially human. It gradually changes everything mineral into warmth ether, everything vegetable to the gaseous, airy or vaporous state, and everything animal—that is, what animals produce in themselves— to the fluid state, creating the solid, organized form of the fully human element. Those are the tendencies inherent in metabolism. And the metabolism is consequently something of remarkable interest.

If we follow the metabolism all the way through to the breathing process, we find that man releases carbon, an element to be found everywhere in the human organism. This is sought out by oxygen and changed into carbon dioxide, which is then exhaled. Carbon dioxide is a compound of carbon and oxygen. The oxygen drawn in through breathing seeks out the carbon and absorbs it; carbon dioxide, the compound formed of oxygen and carbon, is then exhaled. But before it is exhaled, carbon becomes the benefactor, so to speak, of the human organism. Combining with oxygen, and therefore as it were combining what the blood circulation brings about with what the breathing then makes of the blood circulation, carbon becomes the benefactor of the human organization; for, before it leaves the human organization, it lets ether stream out everywhere in the organism. Physiologists merely state that carbon is exhaled with the carbon dioxide. This, however, is only one side of the whole process. Man exhales carbon dioxide; but, due to the process of exhalation, ether is left behind everywhere in the organism; it is left by the carbon when it is claimed by the oxygen. This ether penetrates into man's etheric body, and it is this ether, continually produced by the carbon, which makes the human organization capable of opening itself to spiritual influences, of absorbing astral and etheric impulses from the cosmos. The ether left behind by carbon attracts the cosmic impulses which in turn impose form principles on man. They prepare the nervous system, for example, so that it can be the bearer of thoughts. The ether must continually be present in our senses, in our eyes, for example, so that they may be able to see, to receive the outer light ether. Thus we are indebted to carbon for the supply of ether within us that enables us to come into contact with the outside world.

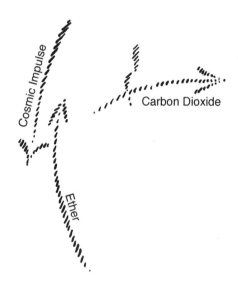

The metabolic system paves the way for all this. But as a human system the metabolic system is so much part of the whole cosmos that it could not exist on its own. It could not exist in isolation. This is why it was only the third system to develop. The first beginnings of the system of nerves and senses took form in the epoch of old Saturn, the rhythmical system during the epoch of old Sun, and the human metabolic system only became possible once the other two systems had come into existence. It could not exist on its own. Leaving voluntary movement aside for the moment, the metabolic system is, in the cosmic scheme of things, designed for human nutrition. However, the process of nutrition cannot function independently. Nutrition is necessary to man, but it cannot exist on its own. If we study the human metabolic system in isolation—in the forthcoming lectures you will see how necessary it is for the human organization as a whole—we find it constantly tending to make us ill, in all sorts of ways. The origin of internal diseases—not those caused by external injury—must always be sought in the metabolic system. A rational observation of diseases must therefore start with the metabolic system, and every metabolic phenomenon needs to be addressed with the question: Which route are you taking? When we consider all the phenomena, from taking food into the mouth, the processes to which the food is subjected in the mouth, with certain substances converted into starch, sugar and so on, and the way the salivary amylase enzyme envelops the food in the mouth; when we go on and consider the addition of pepsin in the stomach and then what happens to the products of metabolism as they pass into the lymph vessels and into the blood, we have to look for every individual process that is involved, and their number is legion. In another process the substances are mixed with the secretion from the pancreas, in yet another with the secretions from the gall-bladder, and so on. To each individual process the question must be put: What is it that you really want? And it will answer: On my own I am a process that always makes man ill. Not one metabolic process may be carried to its conclusion in the human constitution, for carried to its conclusion it will make man ill. The human constitution is only healthy when its metabolic processes are checked at a certain stage.

It might at first seem a folly of Creation that something should begin in man which, if not checked halfway, would make him ill; but in the next lectures we shall learn to recognize this as something of the utmost wisdom. For the time being, however, let us study the actual facts, and discover that the separate metabolic processes would, if we were to question their inner nature, answer: 'We are always on the way to making the whole organism ill.' Every metabolic process, if unchecked, causes illness in the organism. If, therefore, metabolism is to exist at all in man, other processes must exist whose beginnings are of an earlier date. These are the circulatory processes. The circulation produces continuous healing processes. So that we may really describe the human being by saying: During the old Moon evolution man first became a patient, but the human constitution is such that the physician preceded the patient. During the epoch of old Sun, man arose as the physician for his own subsequent constitution. It shows great foresight in world evolution that the physician came into existence before the patient, for the patient in man was only added on old Moon. If we are to describe man rightly, we must work backwards from the metabolic to the circulatory processes, including, of course, all the impulses that underlie the circulatory processes. One substance induces quicker, another substance slower circulation in the widest possible sense. We do of course also have minor circulatory systems in us. Take any mineral substance, gold let us say, or copper. Introduced in some way—by mouth, by injection or in some other way—every substance is endowed with the power of influencing the circulation, changing it, restoring it to health, and so on. And what one must know, in order to gain insight into the essential healing processes in man, is what kind of processes every single substance in the world around us triggers in us to change the circulation. Thus one can say that the circulation is a continual process of healing.

You can, if you wish, work this out for yourselves. Recall how I told you that on average we draw eighteen breaths a minute. Here we find a remarkably regular agreement with the cosmos, for the number of breaths we draw in a day corresponds to the circulatory rhythm of the sun in its course through the solar year. The spring equinox of the sun traverses the entire zodiac in 25,920 years. In middle life we draw on average 25,920 breaths a day. The pulse beats are four times as many. The other, more inwardly concentrated circulation is influenced by the metabolism. The breathing cycle reflects our communication with the outside world, our reciprocal relationship with it. This breathing rhythm must continually restrain the circulatory rhythm, so that it remains in its proportion of one to four, otherwise our circulation would come into a quite irregular rhythm, and not the figure of 103,680. Nothing in the cosmos corresponds to this irregular rhythm, and man is severing all connection with the cosmos in this respect. His metabolism is tearing him away from the cosmos and estranging him from it. His breathing rhythm is continually pulling him back into the cosmos. This division and the way the breathing rhythm controls the circulatory rhythm represents the primal healing process that is continually at work in man. In a certain delicate way, every medical treatment must be designed to assist the breathing process (which in a way continues into all parts of the body) so that it can control the circulatory process and bring it back into harmony with the general relationships in the cosmos.

Thus we may say: We pass over from nutrition to healing inasmuch as, from below upwards, man always has the tendency to become ill, and therefore must continually develop the tendency to remain well in his middle organism, the circulatory organism. And the healing impulses that continually arise in our middle organism leave something behind that goes towards the system of nerves and senses in the head. Thus we are brought to the third part of our organism, the system of nerves and senses. What kind of forces do we find in the nerves and senses? We find there the forces that the physician leaves behind in us, so to speak. On the one hand he works down into the metabolism in a healing way. But in doing so he actually does something that is subject to the appraisal of the whole cosmos. I am telling you something that is not fantasy but an absolute reality. The way in which healing processes are continuously working downwards in us calls forth a feeling of pleasure in the higher hierarchies. It constitutes the joy of the higher hierarchies in the earthly world. They look down and continually feel illness arising out of what streams upwards in man from the earthly, from what remains of the earthly attributes of the substances. And they see that the impulses of *forces* that work out of the earthly realm, forces that lie in the air that moves all around and so on, are continually active as processes of healing. This arouses satisfaction in the higher hierarchies.

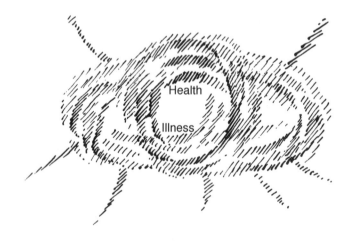

And now try to gain an idea of what can be learned from that cosmic body so very worthy of study, which is situated at the outer boundary of our planetary system. In the centre of this body we find the forces which, if you think of them as concentrated on earth, are illness-inducing forces, and around this same body circulate the forces that bring about healing. Anyone sensitive to such things will see circulating health in the rings of Saturn: it is displayed there in a way that cannot be perceived in what surrounds the earth, because we are embedded in it. A Saturn ring is more than astronomers say it is. It is circulating health, and the inner part of Saturn is the disease-inducing element seen in its purest concentration.

Looking at Saturn, which is situated at the outermost boundary of our planetary system, we see the process at work which we continually bear within ourselves through our metabolism and through our circulatory organism. But we also find, when we look at all this, that our spiritual gaze is directed further to the worlds of the second and the first hierarchy; in the second hierarchy to Kyriotetes, Exusiai and Dynamis, in the first hierarchy to Seraphim, Cherubim and Thrones. If we turn our spiritual eyes to Saturn and its ring, we shall be guided to these higher hierarchies, as they survey with satisfaction the disease-inducing and health-restoring processes.

This satisfaction is in itself a force in the universe. It streams through our system of nerves and senses and creates within it forces for man's spiritual evolution. These are the forces that blossom forth, as it were, from the healing process continually at work in man. Thus in the third place we have the forces of spiritual evolution.

1) Metabolism	Nutrition
2) Circulation	Healing
3) System of nerves and senses	Spiritual evolution

If we now describe man in terms of Saturn, Sun and Moon evolution, we must say: In the first place man is born out of the cosmos as spirit, he then develops in himself the 'healer' who is then able to attend to the cosmic 'patient'. All these work together to produce the human being who lives on earth and is capable of voluntary movement.

Every single branch of human knowledge must be inspired, in a way, by what I have said here. Let us suppose someone wishes to found a system of medicine, a truly rational system of medicine. What would this have to contain? In the first place, naturally, the healing processes. But where will these have to start from? They will have to start with the metabolic processes; everything else is at most a precondition for this— we shall have something further to say about this later. Anatomy, even the finer anatomy, can only be an initial starting point because it is solid and fixed in form. This takes care of its own human nature. But the metabolic processes must first of all be studied in such a way, in a rational system of medicine, that one always perceives the tendency in them towards inducing illness. A modern system of medicine must always take the metabolic system, that is to say the normal metabolic processes, as its point of departure; starting from there one must come to realize the potential that exists for internal diseases to arise from metabolism in the widest sense. Then, adding intimate knowledge of the actions of the rhythmical processes, one will arrive at actual therapy. A modern system of medicine must therefore be founded on a study of the metabolic processes and go on from there to everything that can occur in the sphere of the rhythmical processes in man. Then, I think I may say, a kind of crowning of the whole will be attained by showing how a sound development of man's mental and spiritual potential presupposes a knowledge of what arises from healing forces. You will not find the way to true education today—that is to the art of developing the mental and spiritual potential of human beings in a sound way—unless you start with the healing processes; for these involve nothing other than applying to our middle, rhythmical organization the principle that must be applied in the sphere of pure thought when developing man's mental and spiritual processes.

A skilled teacher must work mentally, spiritually, with the

forces that become healing processes if condensed to the physical or etheric level. The art of education involves a process based on thought, spiritual intent. If I translate this action so that I apply a physical substance or process, where in education I use a mental or spiritual process, the substance or process becomes a medicinal agent. Another way of putting it would be to say that medicine is a metamorphosis into substance of the mental, spiritual way of working with a human being in education. If you call to mind the way in which I indicated this in the teachers' course given some time ago for English visitors,* you will note that I emphasized the fact that the work of the teacher is the beginning of a kind of general human therapy; and I showed how educational measures of one kind or another can in later life be the cause of metabolic deposits giving rise to illness, or of irregular metabolism. So that what the teacher does, projected downwards, results in therapy. And the antithesis of this therapy—what works from below upwards—are the metabolic processes.

Here you also see why a system of medicine today must be born out of a knowledge of man as a whole. And this is possible. Many people feel that this is so. But nothing can really be achieved until such a system is actually developed. It is one of the prime essentials today. If you look at modern textbooks of medicine, you will see that, with the rarest exceptions, they do not take their start from the metabolic system. But this must be the point of departure, otherwise one does not learn to know the real nature of illness.

You see, processes of nutrition can actually pass over into processes of healing, these into mental and spiritual processes, and then back again into processes of healing. Or, if mental and spiritual processes are the direct cause of metabolic disorders, they are entering a state where they need

---

*Rudolf Steiner. *Soul Economy and Waldorf Education*. Rudolf Steiner Press, London 1986.

to be healed by the middle organization of man. All these things closely interact and overlap in man, and the whole human organization is in a state of continual and wonderful metamorphosis. Take, for example, the processes inherent in the whole wonderful circulation of the human blood. What kind of processes are these?

To begin with, separating it entirely from the rest of the human organism, let us gain an idea of the blood as it flows through the veins; let us consider on the one hand the human form, the veins and the adjoining muscular system, skeletal system and so on—that is, all the solid parts of the human body; and on the other hand all the fluid that is in motion. Let us confine ourselves to one fluid, to the blood. There are other fluids as well, but let us confine ourselves to the blood. Now what are the processes continually taking place in this streaming fluidity? The processes that take place in the flowing blood can seize hold, in one direction or another, of elements designed to be walls or supporting structure or anything else that is solid and formed. It means that then something that should be in the blood has entered into the walls of a vessel, into muscle or into bone somewhere or into some other containing organ. What does it become there? It becomes the impulse for inflammatory changes.

What we find here or there as impulses for inflammatory change is continually to be found as normal process in the flowing blood. Any inflammation that develops represents the displacement of processes normally occurring in the flowing blood to the wrong places, that is, to places where solid matter has been given form. A perfectly normal healthy process has been displaced, moved to a location where it does not belong, and becomes a process that induces illness. Certain diseases of the nervous system consist in just this, that the nervous system, which in its whole organization is the polar opposite of the blood system, is subjected to invasion by processes that are normal to the blood. If the processes that are normal in the blood stream invade the nerve pathways in even the slightest degree, the nerves are subject to the initial stages of inflammation and this can develop into the different forms of diseases of the nervous system.

I have said that the processes in the nerves are totally different from those in the blood; they are the antithesis of each other. In the blood one has processes that go in the direction of the phosphorus principle, and if these take hold of tissues that enclose the blood or are adjacent to it, they cause inflammatory conditions. If you study the processes that occur in the nervous pathways and what happens when these stray into adjacent organs, or also into the blood, you get the tendency to tumour development in man. If this is transmitted to the blood, so that the blood supplies the other organs in an unhealthy way, tumours may develop. Any tumour formation is a metamorphosed nerve-related process that is in the wrong place in the human organism.

What runs in the nerve must remain in the nerve, what runs in the blood must remain in the blood. If what belongs in the blood enters into adjacent tissues, inflammation results. If what belongs to the nerve enters into adjacent tissues, all kinds of lesions develop that are commonly referred to as tumours.

The right rhythm must exist between the processes in the nervous system and those in the blood system. Not only do we have the breathing rhythm in contrast with the blood rhythm quite generally, but we also have subtle processes in the circulating blood that become inflammatory processes when they go beyond the blood. These subtle processes must be in a certain rhythmical relationship with the processes in the adjacent nerves, just as breathing must have a relationship with blood circulation. The moment the relationship between blood rhythm and nerve rhythm is disturbed it must be restored.

Here again, you see, we come into the domain of therapy

and of healing processes. All this serves to show you how everything must be present in man, how above all an element of illness must be present so that in another situation it may become an element of health; it is merely that the wrong process has taken it to the wrong place. For if it did not exist at all, man could not exist either. Man could not exist if he were unable to get inflammations, for the inflammation-inducing forces must continually be present in the blood. This was what I meant when I kept saying that everything one gains in the way of knowledge must be won from a real knowledge of man. Here you see why an education carried out in an up-in-the-air, abstract fashion is really something absurd. Education must in fact always start from certain pathological processes in man, and from the possibility of curing them.

If one understands a disease of the brain and the means by which it may be cured, the treatment used for the brain is, at a coarser level—in other respects it is of course refined, but seeing that it is a physical process I am calling it 'coarse' in this case—exactly what must also be applied in education. So if we ever came to found a genuine training college for teachers, we should really teach elements of pathology and therapy; this would first of all school their thinking through things that are more apparent, because they are more rooted in physical substance, and thus prepare for the things they need to grasp in the field of education. On the other hand, nothing is more useful for therapy, and particularly the treatment of internal diseases, than to know the effect of one thing or another in the field of education. If the bridge can be found to the realm of physical substance, then the way in which children should be treated in education will also point to the medical remedy.

If, for example, one finds the right educational means of treating certain signs of lethargy in children that originate in disorders of the digestive system, one develops quite remarkable inner faculties. This happens only, of course, if one enters into education in a really living way, and does not merely work superficially, preferring to spend the evening at the local pub once school is over, forgetting anything that happens in the classroom. The way in which one treats a lethargic child develops an eye for the whole working of the head processes and the whole interrelationship between head processes and abdominal processes. On the other hand, one may study mineralogy and the processes that take place in copper when it gives rise to this or that formation in the earth. It is almost the case then, that in everything copper does as it develops into one copper ore or another, one perceives things that make one say: Look, the copper force is doing in the earth exactly what you as a teacher are doing with a boy or girl! In the copper processes one literally sees a reflection of what one is doing. And it is extraordinarily fascinating for a teacher to develop an intuitive, instinctive clarity of feeling in regard to what he is doing and then have the delight of going out into the world of nature and realizing that nature is actually acting just like a teacher out there, but on a large scale. Wherever something harmful might result from some lime process, a copper process is somehow brought into it. Yes, these copper processes, these ore-forming processes that are part of all the processes that occur on earth, continuously also bring healing.

It is a delight to find pyrites ores, or something else, and be able to say: Yes, this is exactly the same as when a patient receives the right treatment. But here the treatment is given by the spirits of nature, from the hierarchies down to the elemental spirits which I have spoken to you about. They act as healers for all the processes that can cause disorder and disease in life. This is in fact nothing more than reading from nature. If one sees what happens outside, if one turns to one substance or another as a medicine, or makes it into a medicine, one has only to ask oneself: Where does iron or another metal appear in the veins of the earth? Study their environment and you will always find that wherever something metallic appears that has undergone some natural reaction or process, you have a healing process. Take it, continue it on into the human organism and you will create a therapy that nature has demonstrated to you in the world outside.

Yes, any walk in the world outside is in reality a true education in all questions of nutrition, of healing, of the spiritual; for in the world of nature illness is continually being induced and is continually being cured. They are there outside, the great cosmic processes of healing. We must only apply them to man. This is the wonderful interworking of macrocosm and microcosm. What I have said to some of you in one form or another is indeed profoundly true:

> To find and know yourself,
> Look all around you in the world.
> To find and know the world,
> Look into all the depths within yourself.

You can, however, apply this to everything. To heal man, look all around you in the world, see how the world evolves healing processes in all directions. To know the secrets of the world in the processes of illness and healing, look into all the depths of human nature. You can apply this to every aspect of man's being. To be able to do so, however, you must direct your gaze outwards to the great world of nature and see man in a living relationship with this great world.

People today have accustomed themselves to something different. They depart as far from nature as possible. They do something that shuts off their own sight from nature, for when they put the object they wish to examine on a little stand under a lens, the eye then does not look out into nature but into the lens. Sight itself is cut off from nature. They call this a microscope. In some respect it may well be called a nulloscope, for it shuts one off from the great world of nature.

People do not know that to put something under a lens and magnify it is the same for spiritual knowledge as if the same thing were to happen in nature. Just think, if you take some minute particle of a human being and enlarge it under the microscope, you are doing to it what you would be doing to the human individual if you were to stretch him and tear him apart. You would be an even worse monster than Procrustes* if you would stretch and tear the human being apart to enlarge him the way that minute particle is enlarged under the microscope. But do you believe that you would still have that person before you? There is of course no question of this. Nor do you have the truth there under your microscope. Truth that has been magnified is no longer the truth; it is an illusory image. We must not depart from nature and imprison our own sight. For other purposes, this can of course be useful; but for a true knowledge of man it is immensely misleading.

Knowledge of man in the true sense must be sought in the way we have indicated. Starting from the processes of nutrition it must take us to the healing processes and then on to the processes of human and world education in the widest sense. Or we can put it like this: from nutrition through healing to civilization and culture. Look out into the world to find everything that is a basis and foundation for the physical processes concentrated in nutrition in man; for the healing processes that arise from what is in continuous circulation, concentrated in man in the rhythmical processes; for that which comes down from above and in man is concentrated through the processes that occur in the nerves and senses. Thus the world arises and reveals itself in three stages.

This is what I wished to give you in the first place as a kind of foundation. We can now build further on it. We shall see

---

*In Greek mythology, mad Procrustes kept a lodging house near Athens. He made his guests fit his bed—if they were too long he would cut off their feet or their head, if too short he would stretch them on the rack.

how, from such points of departure, we can actually progress to the way to manage this, as it were, in practical life; and from there we can pass on to a knowledge of the hierarchies.

Lecture 11

10 November 1923

You will have gathered from what has been said so far that man's relation to his environment is very different from what modern minds often conceive. It is so easy to think that what exists in man's surroundings, what belongs to the mineral, plant and animal kingdoms and is then taken into the body, that these external material processes which are investigated by the physicist, the chemist and so on, simply continue on in the same way in man himself. There can, however, be no question of this for one must be clear that inside the human skin and its processes everything is different from outside it, that the world inside differs entirely from the world outside. As long as one is not aware of this, one will continually assume that what is examined in a retort, or investigated in some other way, is continued on inside the human organism; and the human organism itself will simply be regarded as a more complex system of retorts.

You need only recall what I said in yesterday's lecture, that everything mineral within man must be transformed until it reaches the condition of warmth ether. This means that everything of a mineral nature which enters into the human organism must be so far metamorphosed, so far changed that, at least for a certain period of time, it becomes pure warmth, becomes one with the warmth which man develops as his own individual temperature independent of the temperature of his environment. No matter whether it is salt or some other mineral that we absorb, in one way or another it must assume the form of warmth ether, and it must do this before it is used to build the living organism.

It is utter nonsense to imagine that some mineral from the outside world would simply transfer itself into the human body and make up some part of the skeletal system, the teeth, etc. Before anything can be part of the human form it must have gone through the completely volatile warmth ether stage and then have been transformed again into a part of the living form of the human organism.

But something quite different is also connected with this: solid substance loses its solid form when it is changed in the mouth into fluid and is then further transformed into the condition of warmth ether. It also gradually loses weight as it passes over into the fluid form and becomes more and more estranged from the earthly; but only when it has ascended to the warmth etheric form is it fully prepared to absorb into itself the spiritual which comes from above, which comes from cosmic breadths.

Thus, if you would gain an idea of how a mineral substance is utilized in man, you must say the following.* There is the mineral substance; this mineral substance enters into man. Within man, passing through the fluid state, and so on, it is transformed into warmth ether. Now it is warmth ether. This warmth ether has a strong disposition to absorb into itself what radiates inwards, streams inwards, as forces from world spaces, from the breadths of the cosmos. Thus it takes into itself the forces of the universe. And these forces of the universe now become the spiritual forces which here imbue warmth-ether-ized earthly matter with spirit. And only then, with the help of this warmth-etherized earthly substance, does there enter into the body what the body needs to take shape and form.

So you see if, in the old sense, we designate heat or warmth as fire we can say: What man absorbs in the way of mineral

---

* A diagram was drawn.

substance is taken up to the level where it becomes of the nature of fire in him. And what is of the nature of fire has the disposition to take up into itself the influences of the higher hierarchies; and then this fire streams back again into all man's internal regions, and resolidifies to provide the material basis for the individual organs. Nothing that human beings take into themselves remains as it is; nothing remains earthly. Everything, and specifically everything that comes from the mineral kingdom, is so far transformed that it can take into itself the spiritual and cosmic; it then resolidifies into the earthly condition with the help of this.

Take a fragment of calcium phosphate from a bone, for instance. This is in no way the calcium phosphate which you find outside in nature, or which, let us say, you produce in the laboratory. It is the calcium phosphate which, while it arose from what was absorbed from outside, could only take part in creating the human physical form with the help of the forces which penetrated it during the time when it was changed into the warmth ether condition.

This, you see, is why man needs substances of the most diverse kinds during the course of his life in order to be able, in accordance with the way he is organized at each particular age, to transform what is lifeless into the condition of warmth ether. A child is as yet quite unable to change what is lifeless into the warmth etheric condition; he has not enough strength in his organism. He must drink the milk which is still so nearly akin to the human organism in order to bring it into the condition of warmth ether and apply its forces to carrying out the truly extensive shaping and moulding that is necessary during the years of childhood to produce the human form. One only gains insight into the nature of man when one knows that everything which is taken in from outside must be worked on and thoroughly transformed. Thus, if you take some external substance and wish to test its value for human life you simply cannot do this by means of ordinary chemistry. You must know how much force the human organism has to exert in order to bring an external mineral substance to the fleeting condition of warmth ether. If it is unable to do this, the external mineral substance is deposited and becomes heavy earth matter before it has passed over into warmth; it remains foreign inorganic matter and is deposited in the tissues.

This may happen, for example, when the human being is not able to bring a substance that—though organic in origin—appears mineralized in him, namely sugar, to the tenuous condition of warmth ether. It is then deposited in the organism without ever having reached the condition which it must achieve if the whole organism is to have part in everything it contains, and the very serious condition of diabetes develops. In the case of every substance one must therefore consider to what degree the human organism can transmute lifeless substance into warmth substance, whether the nature of that substance is already lifeless, as when we eat common salt, or whether it becomes so, as with sugar. In warmth substance, the organism, which is rooted in the earth, finds its connection with the spiritual cosmos.

Every deposit in man which remains untransmuted—as in diabetes—signifies that the human being does not find the connection with the spiritual of the cosmos for the substances present within him. This is only a special application of the general axiom that whatever approaches man from outside must be entirely worked over and transformed within him. And if we wish to look after a person's health it is of paramount importance to see to it that nothing enters into him that will remain as it was, nothing that cannot be dealt with by the human organism and transformed even if it is only quite minor in degree. This is not only the case in regard to substances; it is also the case, for instance, in regard to forces.

External warmth—the warmth we feel when we touch things, the external warmth in the air—this, when taken up by the human organism, must be so transformed that the inner warmth is at a different level from the warmth outside. External warmth must be somewhat transformed in us, so that this external warmth, in which we are not present, is laid hold of by the human organism, right down to the least particle of warmth.

Now imagine that I go somewhere cold, and because the cold is too intense, or because moving air or a draught creates fluctuations in temperature, I am not in a position to change the world warmth into my own individual warmth quickly enough. This means that I run the danger of being warmed by the world's warmth from outside like a piece of wood, or a stone. This should not be. I should not be exposed to the danger of external warmth flowing into me as though I were merely some object. At every moment, I must be able to lay hold of the warmth from the boundary of my skin inwards and make it my own. If I am not in a position to do this I catch a cold.

That is the inner process of catching a cold. To catch a cold is a poisoning by external temperature, of which the organism has not taken possession.

You see, everything in the external world is poison for man, actual poison, and it only becomes of service to him when, through his individual forces, he lays hold of it and makes it his own. For only from man himself do forces ascend to the higher hierarchies in a human way; whereas outside man they remain with the elemental nature beings, with the elemental spirits. In the case of man this wonderful transformation must happen so that the elemental spirits in the human organization may give over their work to the higher hierarchies. For the mineral in man this can only occur when it is absolutely and entirely transformed into warmth ether.

Let us look at the plant world. Truly this plant world has something of manifold enchantment to us when we begin to contemplate the plant cover of the earth with the eye of the spirit. We go out into a meadow or a wood. We dig up, let us say, a plant with its root. If we bring spiritual perception to bear upon what we have dug up, we find a wonderfully magical complex. The root shows itself as something of which we can say that it has become entirely earthly. Yes, a plant root—the coarser the more so—is really something terribly earthly. A root—especially a turnip root, for instance—always reminds one of a particularly well-fed alderman. Oh, yes, it is so; the root of a plant is extremely smug and self-satisfied. It has absorbed the salts of the earth and feels a deep sense of gratification at having soaked up the earth. In the whole sphere of earthly existence there is no more absolute expression of satisfaction than such a turnip root; it is representative of root nature.

On the other hand let us look at the flower. When we observe a flower with the eye of the spirit we cannot help but experience it to be like our own soul when it cherishes the tenderest desires. Only look at a spring flower; it is a breath of longing, the embodiment of a wish. And something wonderful streams forth over the world of flowers that surrounds us, if only our soul perception is delicate enough to be open to it.

In spring we see the violet, maybe the daffodil, the lily-of-the-valley, or some plants with yellow flowers, and we are seized by the feeling that these spring-flowering plants would say to us: O man, how pure and innocent can be the desires which you direct towards the spiritual! Spiritual desire nature, desire nature bathed, as it were in godliness, breathes from every spring flower.

And when the later flowers appear—let us go straight to the other extreme, let us take the autumn crocus—can one behold the autumn crocus with soul perception without having a slight feeling of shame? Does it not warn us that our desires can become impure, that our desires can be imbued with every kind of corruption? It is as though the autumn crocuses spoke to us from all sides, as if they would continually whisper to us: Consider the world of your desires, O man; how easily you can become a sinner!

Looked at thus, the plant world is the mirror of human conscience in external nature. Nothing more poetical can be imagined than the thought of this voice of conscience, which in us comes forth as though from a single point, distributed over the many different kinds of flowers that speak to the soul during the seasons of the year in the most manifold ways. The plant world reveals itself as the outspread mirror of conscience if we know how to look at it aright.

If we bear this in mind it becomes of special significance for us to look at the flowers and picture how the flower is really our longing for the light-filled spaces of the universe, how it literally grows upwards in order to send the desires of the earth streaming towards the light-filled spaces of the universe, and how on the other hand the substantial root fetters the plant to the earth; how it is the root which continually wrests those celestial desires away from the plant, wishing to change them into earthly ease and satisfaction.

And we learn to understand why this is so when, in the evolutionary history of the earth, we meet the fact that what is present in the root of a plant has invariably been laid down in the time when the moon was still one with the earth.

In the time when the moon was still one with the earth, the forces anchored in the moon were so powerful in the body of the earth that they hardly allowed the plant to become anything but root. When the moon was still with the earth, and the earth still had a quite different substance, the root element spread itself out and worked downwards with great power. We can picture the downward thrust of the plant's root nature spreading out powerfully, while up above the plant merely peeped out into the cosmos. We could say that the plants sent their shoots out into the cosmos like delicate little hairs. Thus we can sense that while the moon was still with the earth this moon element, the moon's forces contained in the earth's body itself, fettered the plant's nature to the earthly. And what was then transmitted to the being of the plant remains as a predisposition in the nature of the root.

After the moon had left the earth, however, a longing for the light-filled spaces of the universe unfolded in what had previously existed only as tiny little shoots peeping out into the universe; and now the floral element developed. So that the departure of the moon was a kind of liberation, a real liberation for the plants.

But here we must also bear in mind that everything earthly has its origin in the spiritual. During the old Saturn period—you need only take the description which I gave in my *Occult Science*—the earth was entirely spiritual; it existed only in the element of heat or warmth ether, it was all spirit. It is out of the spiritual that the earthly was formed.

And now let us contemplate the plant. In its form it bears the living memory of evolution. In its root nature it bears the process of becoming earthly, of assuming the physical and material. If we look at the root of a plant we also discern that it says something to us, namely, that its existence only became possible because the earthly and material evolved out of the spiritual. Scarcely, however, was the earth relieved of its moon element than the plant again strove back to light-filled spaces.

When we consume the plant as nourishment we give it the opportunity of carrying further, in the right way, what it began outside in nature, striving back not only to light-filled spaces, but to the spirit-filled spaces of the cosmos. This is why, as I said yesterday, we must take the plant substance within us to the point where it becomes aeriform, or gaseous, so that the plant may follow its longing for the wide spaces of light and spirit.

I go out into a meadow. I see how the flowers strive towards the light. Man consumes the plant, but within him he has a world entirely different from the one outside. Within him he can bring to fulfilment the longing which, outside, the plant expresses in its flowers. Spread abroad in nature we see the desire world of the plants. We eat the plants. We drive this longing towards the spiritual world within us. We must therefore raise the plants into the sphere of the air so that in this lighter realm they may be enabled to strive towards the spiritual.

The plant undergoes a strange and peculiar process in us. When we eat plant food the following occurs: If we have the root here below,* and above what strives through the leaf to the flower, then in this transformation into the airy condition we have to experience inwardly a total reversal of plant nature. The root, which is fettered to the earth for the very reason that it lives in the earth, strives upwards; it strives upwards towards the spiritual with such power that it leaves the striving of the flower behind it. It is actually as if you were to picture the plant unfolding below like this and the lower can then be pushed up through the centre, so that the upper becomes the lower and the lower the upper (demonstration with a hand-kerchief). The plant reverses itself completely. The part that has already achieved the level of the flower has had enjoyment of the light in its material striving, has brought the material up into the sphere of the light. For this, it must now suffer the punishment of remaining below. The root has been the slave of the earthly; but, as you can see from Goethe's theory of the metamorphosis of plants, it bears the plant's whole nature within it. It now strives upwards.

Inveterate sinners generally want to remain as they are. But the root of a plant, which as long as it is bound to the earth makes the impression of a well-fed alderman, is transformed and strives upwards immediately when it has been eaten by man; whereas that which has taken physical matter into the sphere of light, the flower, must remain down below. Hence in what belongs to the root element of the plant we have

---

* A diagram was drawn.

something which, when it is eaten, strives upwards towards the human head and really does this out of its inherent nature, while what lies in the direction of the flower remains in the lower regions; within the total metabolism it does not go up as far as the head process.

Thus we have the remarkable, the wonderful drama that when man consumes some kind of plant or vegetable—he need not eat the whole plant, because in each single part the whole plant is inherent (I refer you again to Goethe's theory of metamorphosis)—it transforms itself within him into air which, like an inverted plant, grows and flowers from above downwards.

In times when such things were known through ancient, instinctive clairvoyance, people looked at the external constitution of plants in order to see whether they were such as could be beneficial to the human head, whether the root already gave a strong indication of a longing for the spiritual. For, when digestion is completed, what we have eaten of such a plant will seek out the head and penetrate it, so that it may there strive upwards towards the spiritual cosmos and enter into the necessary connection with it.

In the case of plants that are strongly imbued with astrality, for example peas and beans, even the fruit will remain in the lower human organism and be unwilling to rise up to the head, thus producing a heavy sleep and dulling the brain on waking. The Pythagoreans wished to be clear thinkers and not involve digestion in the functions of the head. This is why they forbade the eating of beans.

You see, therefore, that from what happens in nature we can divine something of nature's relation to man, and to what happens in man. If one pursues spiritual initiation science, one simply cannot imagine how materialistic science gets to grips with human digestion (matters are of course different in regard to a cow's digestion—about this, too, we shall have something further to say later) by stating that plants are simply ingested. They are not simply ingested but completely spiritualized. The plant form in itself is inverted, so that the lower turns into the upper and the upper into the lower. No greater transformation can be imagined. And man immediately becomes ill if he eats even the smallest quantity of a plant where the lowest is not changed into the uppermost, and the uppermost into the lowest.

From this you will realize that man bears nothing in himself which is not worked on by the spirit; all substances taken into the organism must first be given a form which will enable the spirit to influence them.

Turning now to the animal world, we must be clear that in the first place the animal does have a digestive system and that plant substance is ingested. Let us take the herbivorous animals. The animal world takes the plant world into itself. This again is a very complicated process, for when the animal ingests the plant it does not have the human form to set against the plant. Within the animal, the plant cannot turn the above into the below and the below into the above, for the animal has its vertebral column parallel with the surface of the earth. This means that in the case of the animal what should happen in digestion is thrown into complete disorder. What is below strives upwards, and what is above strives downwards, but the whole process gets dammed up in itself, so that animal digestion is something essentially different from human digestion. In animal digestion, what lives in the plant dams itself up. And the result of this is that in the animal, plant nature is given the promise: 'You may indulge your longing for the breadths of the cosmos'—but the promise is not kept. The plant is repulsed back to earth again.

Through the fact, however, that the plant is cast back to earth in the animal organism, there immediately penetrate into the plant not cosmic spirits with their forces—as with man in whom the reversal takes place—but certain elemental spirits. These are elemental spirits of fear and anxiety, the bearers of fear and anxiety. Spiritual perception can follow this remarkable process. The animal itself enjoys its nourishment, enjoys it with inner satisfaction; and while the food stream goes in one direction, a stream of fear from elemental spirits of fear goes in the other. Through the animal's digestive tract there continually flows along the alimentary canal the satisfaction felt in the taking of food, and in opposition to the digestive process goes a terrible stream of fear that comes from elemental spirits.

This is what animals leave behind them when they die. When animals die—not those species, perhaps, that I have already described in another context but nevertheless including some four-footed mammals for instance—when these animals die there also dies, or rather comes to life in their dying, a being which is entirely composed of anxiety. With the animal's death, fear is released, comes to life. In the case of beasts of prey, this fear is actually part of their enjoyment of the food. The beast of prey, which tears its prey to pieces, devours the flesh with satisfaction. And towards this satisfaction in the consumption of meat there streams fear, the fear which the herbivorous animal only gives off when it dies, but which already streams out from the beast of prey during its lifetime. The astral bodies of such animals as lions and tigers are therefore riddled with fear which they do not feel during their lifetime but which after death these animals drive back because it runs counter to their feeling of satisfaction. Thus carnivorous animals have an after-life in their group soul which must be said to be a much more terrible kamaloka than anything which can be experienced by man, and this simply on account of their intrinsic nature.

Naturally you must regard these things as being experienced in quite a different consciousness. If you took the materialistic view again, and began to imagine what the beast of prey must experience by putting yourself in its place, thinking: What would such a kamaloka be like for me? and were then to judge the beast of prey according to what such a kamaloka might be for you, then you are of course materialistic, indeed animalistic, for you transpose yourself into animal nature. These things must of course be understood if one is to comprehend the world; but we must not put ourselves, with the consciousness we have, in their place, as when the materialist puts himself and the whole world into the category of lifeless matter.

This brings us to something about which I can only speak on a soul level, for anthroposophy should never campaign for anything, should never advocate either one thing or another, but should only present the truth. The conclusions people draw for their own lives are their own personal affair. Anthroposophy does not lay down rules, but puts forward truths. For this reason I shall never, even for fanatics, lay down any kind of law based on what an animal produces from its plant food. No dogmatic commands shall be given in regard to vegetarianism, meat-eating and so on, for these things must be a matter of personal judgement entirely and it is really only in the sphere of individual experience that they have value. I mention this in order to avoid giving people the idea that anthroposophy entails advocating this or that kind of diet. What it actually does is enable people to understand any form of diet.

What I really wished to show was that we must work on the mineral until it becomes warmth ether in order that it may absorb the spiritual; then, after the mineral has absorbed the spiritual, man can be built up by it. I mentioned that when the human being is still very young he does not yet have the strength to work on what is entirely mineral and convert it into warmth ether. Some of the work has been done for him when he drinks milk. Milk has already undergone preliminary changes which make the process of transformation to warmth ether easier. In a child the milk with its forces flows up quickly into the head and can there give rise to form-developing impulses in a way which the child can make use of, for the whole organization of the child proceeds from the head.

If at a later age man wishes to retain these form-developing forces, it is not good to promote them by drinking milk. In the case of the child what ascends into the head is able, by means of the forces of the head which are present until the change of teeth, to radiate form principles into the whole body; in an older person the process is no longer present. In later age, the whole of the rest of the organism must radiate form-giving forces. And these form-giving forces for the whole organism are particularly strengthened in their impulses when one eats something which works in quite another way than is the case with the head.

You see, the head is entirely enclosed. Within this head are the impulses used in childhood for the shaping of the body. In the rest of the body we have bones within and the form-giving forces outside, so that the form-developing forces must be stimulated from outside. While we are children these form-giving forces in the head are stimulated when we give milk to the human being. When we are no longer children these forces are no longer there. What should we do then so that these form-giving forces may be stimulated more from outside?

It would obviously be a good thing to be able to have in our outer form what is accomplished within by the head, enclosed as it is inside the skull. It would be good if what the head does inside itself could be accomplished from somewhere outside. The forces which are there within the head are suited to the consumption of milk; when the milk is there in its etheric transformation it provides a good basis for the development of these head forces. We therefore ought to have something that acts like milk but is not produced within the human being, is instead produced from outside.

Well, there is something existing outside in nature which is a head without an enclosing skull and in which the same forces act from outside that work inside the head in children who need milk and must even create it anew (the child must first bring milk into the warmth etheric condition and so create it anew).

A stock of bees is really a head open on all sides. What the bees are doing is actually the same as what the head does within itself. The hive we give them is at most a support. The bees' activity, however, is not enclosed but produced from outside. In a stock of bees we have under external spiritual influence the same thing as we have under spiritual influence inside the head. We have honey inside the bee hive and when we eat and enjoy honey it gives us the form-giving forces that must now be provided more from outside, with the same strength and power that milk gives us for our head during the years of childhood.

Thus while we are still children we consume milk to strengthen the form-giving forces in a process that comes from the head; if at a later age we still need form-giving forces we must eat honey. Nor do we need to eat it in tremendous quantities—it is only a question of absorbing its forces.

Thus by fully understanding the outer world of nature one learns how forces that help development must be introduced into human life. And if we would conceive a land where there are beautiful children and beautiful old people, what kind of a land would this be? It would be a 'a land flowing with milk and honey'. So you see ancient instinctive vision was in no way wrong when it said that the lands people longed for were those flowing with milk and honey.

Many such simple sayings contain the profoundest wisdom and there is really no more beautiful experience than first to make every possible effort to experience the truth, and then to find some ancient holy saying abounding in deep wisdom, such as 'a land flowing with milk and honey'. That is indeed a rare land, for in it there are only beautiful children and beautiful old people.

You see, to understand man presupposes understanding the world of nature. To understand the world of nature provides the basis for the understanding of man. And here the lowest spheres of the material always lead up to the highest spheres of the spiritual: the kingdoms of nature—mineral, animal, vegetable—at the one, the lowest pole; above, at the other pole, the hierarchies themselves.

Lecture 12

11 November 1923

Once we realize that external nature is transformed inside the human organism, and this in so radical a way that the mineral, for example, must be lifted into the warmth ether, we will also know that all that lives in man, in the human organization, is connected with the spiritual. If we follow the ideas that commonly arise in connection with the illustrations seen in conventional textbooks of anatomy and physiology and imagine man to be a solid body that takes into itself the products of external nature and that these remain almost unchanged in the human body, then we will always suffer from the lack of a necessary bridge spanning between what exists in man as part of the physical world, and the world with which he is connected through his essential soul nature.

At first we shall be unable to find any connection between the skeletal and muscular systems, which we imagine to be solid physical substance, and, for instance, the moral world order. It will be said that the one is simply physical nature and that the other is something radically different from physical nature. But when we are clear about the fact that all forms of substantiality are present in man and that everything must go through a stage where it is more volatile than muscles and bones are, we shall come to realize that this more volatile and etheric substance can enter into connection with the impulses of the moral world order.

This is the point of departure for our present considerations, and for then tracing the connection between man and the higher realms of the spiritual in the cosmos, the beings whom we have called the beings of the higher hierarchies. In the earlier lectures we took our starting point more from the world of nature. Today, however, let us take our start from the spiritual and moral impulses that are active in the human realm.

In modern civilization terms such as 'spiritual' and 'moral' have more or less become routine, conventional ideas. The pure original feeling for the moral and spiritual element in human nature has increasingly been lost. The whole approach to education in modern civilization leads man to ask: What is customary? What has convention ordained? What is the code? What is the law?—and so on. Less account is taken of what comes forth as impulses and is rooted in the part of man which is often relegated in a vague way to conscience. This inner directing of oneself, this determining of one's own goals, is something that has increasingly been lost in modern civilization. Hence the spiritual and moral has finally become little more than convention and tradition.

Earlier world conceptions, particularly those which were sustained by instinctive clairvoyance, brought forth moral impulses from man's inner nature. Moral impulses still exist, but today they have become tradition. And we need to realize the extent to which this is true. Of course nothing whatever is implied here against traditional morality—but only think of the Ten Commandments and how old they are. They are taught as commands recorded in ancient times. Is it to be expected today that something might spring forth from the primary, elemental sources of human nature which could be compared to what once arose as the Decalogue, the Ten Commandments?

From what source does the moral and spiritual arise, which binds people together in a social way, which knits the threads uniting person to person? There is only one true source of the moral and spiritual in mankind, and this is what we may call mutual understanding and a love for humanity that is based on this human understanding. Wheresoever we may look for the source of moral and spiritual impulses in mankind, in so far as these play a role in social life, it will invariably turn out that such impulses have sprung forth in their pure form from human understanding and human love. These are the actual driving force for moral and spiritual impulses in the social sphere. And fundamentally speaking, in so far as he is a spiritual being, man lives from one thing only when he is with other human beings—from developing human love and understanding.

Here you may ask a significant question, a question that is indeed not always voiced but should indeed be on the tip of every tongue, particularly in regard to what has just been said: If human love and understanding are the real impulses on which communal life depends, how does it come about that exactly the reverse, lack of understanding and hatred of our fellow human beings, appear in our social order?

This is a question with which initiates, more than anyone else, have always concerned themselves. In every age in which initiation science arose as an impulse, this very question was regarded as one of their most vital concerns. When this initiation science was still a primal impulse, however, it possessed certain means of finding the solution to the problem. But if one looks at conventional science today, one is forced to ask: As the god-created soul is naturally predisposed to human understanding and human love, why are these qualities not active as a matter of course in the social order? Whence come human hatred and lack of human understanding? Now, if we are unable to look for them in the realm of soul and spirit, it follows that we must look for them in the physical realm.

Yes—but in modern conventional science the answer as to what the physical, bodily nature of man is tends to be: blood, nerves, muscles, bones. No matter how long one studies a bone, if one only does so with the eye of present-day science, one will never be able to say this bone is what leads man astray into hatred. And to whatever degree one is able to investigate the blood according to the principles by which it is investigated today, one will never be able to say: This blood is what leads man astray into lack of human understanding.

In times when initiation science was a primal impulse matters were certainly quite different. Then one turned one's gaze to the physical, bodily nature of man and perceived it to be the counter-image of what instinctive clairvoyance provided at the level of mind and spirit.

When people speak of the things of the spirit today they refer at most to abstract thoughts; these are what they regard as spiritual. If they find these thoughts too tenuous, all that remains to them is words, and then they do as Fritz Mauthner has done. In his *Critique of Language** he manages to dilute the spirit—already tenuous enough—until it becomes utterly devoid of substance and nothing but abstract ideas. The people who had initiation knowledge irradiated with instinctive clairvoyance did not see the things of the spirit in terms of abstract thought. They saw the things of the spirit as forms and figures, as something that took the form of images, something that was able to speak and resound. The spiritual was alive for those who had that initiation knowledge. And because the spiritual was seen in a living way, the physical— blood and bones—could also be perceived in its spirituality. This initiation knowledge did not include the thoughts and notions that we have today about the skeleton. Today the skeleton is really regarded as something constructed by the calculations of an architect for the purposes of physiology and anatomy. But it is not. The skeleton, as you have seen, is given form by taking mineral substance upwards to the state of warmth ether, so that in the warmth ether the forces of the

---

* Fritz Mauthner (1849–1923), writer and philosopher. *Beiträge zu einer Kritik der Sprache* 1901.

higher hierarchies are able to intervene, and out of this the bones are created.

To one who is able to behold it rightly, the skeleton reveals its spiritual origin. But one who looks at the skeleton in its present form—I mean in the way in which present-day scientists tend to regard it—is like a person standing before a printed page with shapes on it that are letters, but who does not read their meaning because he is unable to read. He does not relate what is expressed in the shape of the letters to what lies behind them; he only describes their shapes. In the same way present-day anatomists and scientists describe the bones as if they were entirely without meaning. What they really reveal, however, is their origin in the spiritual.

And so it is with everything that exists as physical and etheric natural laws. They are written characters from the spiritual world. And we only understand these things rightly when we can comprehend them as written characters proceeding from spiritual worlds.

Now, when we are able to regard the human organism in this way, we become aware of something which belongs to the domain of which the true initiates of all epochs have said: In crossing the threshold into the spiritual world, the first thing one becomes aware of is something terrible, something which at first is by no means easy to bear. Most people wish to take pleasure in what seems to them worthy of attainment. But the fact remains that only by passing through the experience of shock can one learn to know spiritual reality, that is to say true reality. For in regard to the anatomical and physiological human form one will perceive that the spiritual world has built it up out of two elements: moral coldness and hatred.

In our souls we truly possess the predisposition to human love and that moral warmth which understands the other human being. In the solid components of our organism, however, we bear moral coldness. This is the force through which the spiritual world welds, as it were, our physical organism together. We bear in ourselves the impulse of hatred. This derives from the spiritual world to bring about our blood circulation. And whereas we may perhaps go through the world with a very loving soul, with a soul that thirsts for human understanding, we must nevertheless be aware that below in the subconscious, where the soul streams into the physical body and sends its impulses into it, for the very purpose that we may be clothed in a body—coldness has its seat. Though I will just use the word 'coldness' all the time, what I mean is moral coldness, though this can certainly pass over into physical coldness by way of the warmth ether. There below in the subconscious moral coldness and hatred have their seat, and it is easy for man to bring into his soul what is present in his body, so that his soul can, as it were, be infected with lack of human understanding. This is, however, the result of moral coldness and human hatred. Because this is so, man must gradually cultivate in himself moral warmth, that is to say human understanding and love, for these must vanquish what comes from bodily nature.

Now it cannot be denied—this presents itself in all clarity to spiritual vision—that in our age, which began with the fifteenth century and has developed in an intellectualistic way on the one hand and in a materialistic way on the other, much lack of understanding and human hatred has become embedded in human souls. This is so to a greater degree than is supposed. For only when man passes through the gate of death does he become aware of how much lack of understanding, how much hatred, is present in the unconscious. There man detaches his soul and spiritual from his physical, bodily nature. He lays his physical, bodily nature aside. The impulses of coldness, the impulses of hatred, then reveal themselves simply as natural forces, as mere forces of nature.

Let us look at a corpse. Let us even look with spiritual gaze upon the etheric corpse. Here we are looking at something which no longer evokes moral judgement any more than does a plant or a stone. The moral forces which have previously been contained in what is now the corpse have been changed into natural forces. During his lifetime, however, the human being absorbed a great deal from them; this he takes with him through the gate of death. The ego and astral body withdraw, taking with them as they go what remained unnoticed during life because it was always entirely submerged in the physical and etheric bodies. The ego and astral body take with them into the spiritual world all the impulses of human hatred and coldness towards others that have gained access to their souls. As I said, it is only when one sees the human being pass through the gate of death that one perceives how much failure to understand, how much human hatred have been implanted into the individual, particularly in our civilization, by various things about which I shall still have to speak. Human beings of today carry a great deal of these two impulses through the gate of death, a very great deal indeed.

But what man thus carries with him is in fact the spiritual residue of what should exist in the physical, of what should constitute the physical and etheric bodies. In the lack of human understanding and the human hatred which man takes into the spiritual world we have the residue of what really belongs in the physical world. He carries it there in a spiritual way, but to carry it onward through the time between death and a new birth would make him quite unable to progress. At every step in his further evolution between death and a new birth he would stumble if he were obliged to carry further this failure to understand the other individual, this human hatred. In the spiritual world, which is entered by the so-called dead, one continually sees currents that would prevent further development if they continued to act exactly as they are. Where do these currents originate?

To discover this we need only look at modern life. People pass one another by; they pay little heed to the individual nature of others. Are not people today mostly so constituted that each one regards himself as the standard of what is right and proper? And when someone differs from this standard we do not take kindly to him, but rather think that this person should be different. And this usually implies: He should be like me. We are not always aware of this, but it is to be found specifically in human social intercourse.

In the way things manifest today—for instance in the whole manner and form of people's speech—there lies very little understanding of the other person. People bellow out their ideas about how human beings should behave, but this usually means: Everyone should be like me. If someone comes along who is completely different, he is immediately regarded as an enemy, an object for antipathy, though we tend not to be fully conscious of this. There is lack of human understanding, of moral warmth and of love. And to the degree in which these qualities are lacking, moral coldness and human hatred go with man through the gate of death, obstructing his path.

Having gone through the gate of death, however, he finds that his further development is not his own concern alone, but the concern of the whole world order, the wisdom-filled world order. First of all he finds in the other world beings of the third hierarchy, angels, archangels, archai. In the first period after man has passed through the gate of death into the world lying between death and a new birth these beings stoop downward and mercifully take from man the coldness which comes from lack of human understanding. And we see how the beings of the third hierarchy assume the burden of what man carries up to them into the spiritual world in the way I have described, by passing through the gate of death.

It is for a longer period that man must carry with him the remains of human hatred, for this can only be taken from him by grace of the spirits of the second hierarchy, exusiai, kyriotetes, dynamis. They take from him all that remains of human hatred.

And then the human being arrives in the region between death and a new birth where the first hierarchy, seraphim, cherubim, thrones, have their abiding place, which I described in my Mystery Play as the midnight hour of existence in the spirit.* Man would be quite unable to pass through this region of the seraphim, cherubim and thrones without being inwardly annihilated, utterly destroyed, had not the beings of the second and third hierarchies already taken from him in their mercy human lack of understanding, that is to say moral coldness, and human hatred. And so we see how man, in order to find access to the impulses that can contribute to his further development, must at first burden the beings of the higher hierarchies with what he carries up into the spiritual world from his physical and etheric bodies, where it really belongs.

When one has insight into all this, when one sees how this moral coldness exists in the spiritual world, one will also know how to judge the relation between this spiritual coldness and the physical coldness that exists here below. The physical coldness which we find in snow and ice is only the physical image of the moral and spiritual coldness which is there above. If we have them both before us, we can compare them.

While man is being relieved in this way of human misunderstanding and human hatred, one can follow with the spiritual eye how he begins to lose his form, how this form more or less melts away. When someone first passes through the gate of death, to the spiritual vision of Imagination his appearance is still somewhat similar to what it was here on earth. For what a human being bears within him here on earth is in fact just substances in more or less granular form, let us say, in atomistic form; but the human figure itself—that is spiritual.

---

* Rudolf Steiner. *Four Mystery Dramas.* The Soul's Awakening, Scenes 5 and 6. Rudolf Steiner Press, London 1997.

We must really be clear about this. It is sheer nonsense to regard the human form as physical; we must see it as a spiritual form. The physical in it is everywhere present as minute particles. The form, which is only a force body, holds together what would otherwise fall apart into a heap of atoms. If someone were to take any of you by the forelock and extract your form, the physical and also the etheric would collapse like a heap of sand. That these are not just a sandheap, that they are distributed and take on form, stems from nothing physical; it stems from the spiritual. Here in the physical world man goes about as something spiritual. It is senseless to think that man is only a physical being; his form is purely spiritual. The physical in him may almost be likened to a heap of crumbs.

Man, however, still possesses his form when he goes through the gate of death. One sees it shimmering, glittering, radiant with colours. But now he loses first the form of his head; then the rest of his form gradually melts away. Man becomes completely metamorphosed, as though transformed into an image of the cosmos. This occurs during the time between death and a new birth when he comes into the region of the seraphim, cherubim and thrones.

Thus, when one follows the human being between death and a new birth, one at first still sees him, as it were, continue to be active while he gradually loses his form from above downwards. But as the last vestige of him is vanishing away below, something else has evolved: a wonderful spirit form, which is in itself an image of the whole world sphere and at the same time a model of the future head which the human being will bear on his shoulders. Here the human being is involved in an activity wherein not only the beings of the lower hierarchies participate, but also the beings of the highest hierarchy, the seraphim, cherubim and thrones.

What actually takes place? It is the most wonderful thing of which we human beings can possibly conceive. For all that was lower man here in life now passes over into the formation of the future head. As we go about here on earth, we only have our poor head as the organ of our mental images and our thoughts. But thoughts also accompany our chest, thoughts also particularly accompany our limbs. And the moment we cease to think only with the head, but begin to think with our limbs, in that moment the whole reality of karma is opened up to us. We know nothing of our karma because we always think only with that most superficial of organs, our brain. The moment we begin to think with our fingers—and just with our fingers and toes we can think much more brightly than with the nerves of the head—once we have soared up to the possibility of doing so—the moment we begin to think with what has not become entirely material, when we begin to think with the lower man, our thoughts are the thoughts of our karma. When we do not merely grasp with our hand but think with it, then, thinking with our hand, we follow our karma. And even more so with the feet; when we do not only walk but think with our feet, we follow the course of our karma with special clarity. That man is such a dullard on earth—excuse me, but no other word occurs to me—comes from the fact that all his thinking is enclosed in the region of his head. But man can think with his entire being. Whenever we think with our entire being, then for our middle region a whole cosmology, a marvellous cosmic wisdom, becomes our own. And for the lower region and the limb system especially karma becomes our own.

We already do a good deal just by looking at the way a person walks, not in a dull way, but marking the beauty of his step, and what is characteristic in it; or when we allow his hands to make an impression upon us, so that we interpret these hands and think that in every movement of the fingers there lie wonderful revelations of man's inner nature. Yet that is only the least part of what moves as man walks, or takes hold of something with his hand, or just moves his fingers. For it is man's whole moral nature which moves; his destiny moves with him, everything that he is as a spiritual being. And if, after man has passed through the gate of death, we are able to follow how his form dissolves—anything reminiscent of the physical form is first to melt away—there then appears what does indeed resemble his physical structure, but which in its inner nature, its inner being, makes us aware that this is the moral form. This is what happens to man as he approaches the midnight hour of existence and comes into the sphere of the seraphim, cherubim and thrones. We see how this wonderful metamorphosis occurs, how his form melts away. But this is not really the essential point. It looks as though the form would dissolve away, but the truth is that the spiritual beings of the higher worlds are there working together with man. They work with the human beings who are working on themselves and on others with whom they have karmic connections. One human being works on the other. These spiritual beings, then, together with man himself, develop the form he had in his previous earthly life into what will be his form in his next earthly life. Initially this is a spiritual form.

The spirit form will finally connect with the embryo in physical life. But in the spiritual world feet and legs are transformed into the jaw bones, while arms and hands are transformed into cheekbones. The whole lower man is transformed into the spiritual beginnings of what will later be the head. The way in which this metamorphosis is accomplished is, I do assure you, the most wonderful of everything that the world offers to conscious experience. We see at first how an image of the whole cosmos is created, and how this is then condensed and differentiated into the form which the whole moral element attaches to—but only after all that I have mentioned has been taken from it. We see how what was transforms itself into what will be. Now one sees the human being as spirit form journeying back once more to the region of the second hierarchy and then to that of the third hierarchy. Here the metamorphosed spirit form—it is in fact only the basis for the future head—must, as it were, have added to it what will become the future chest organs, the future limbs and metabolic organs. These must be added. Whence come the spiritual impulses to add them?

It is by grace of the beings of the second and third hierarchies, who gathered these impulses together when the human being was on the first half of his journey. They took them from his moral nature; now they bring them back again and shape them into the basis for the rhythmical system and the system of metabolism and limbs. In this later period between death and a new birth man receives the ingredients, the spiritual ingredients, for his physical organism. This spiritual form finds its way into the embryo, and brings to it what now turns into physical and etheric forces. These are, however, only the physical image of what we bear in us from our previous life as lack of human understanding and as human hatred, and from which our limb organization is spiritually formed.

If we wish to see things in this way, we must acquire a manner of feeling and perceiving quite other than that needed in the physical world. For we must be able to look at the things of the spirit that become physical in man in the way I have described; we must be able to bear the knowledge that coldness, moral coldness, lives as physical image in the bones and that moral hatred lives as physical image in the blood. We must learn to look at these matters quite objectively.

It is in fact only when we look into things in this way that we become aware of the fundamental difference between man's inner being and the world of nature outside.

Just consider for a moment the fact I mentioned, namely, that in the flowers of the plant kingdom we see, as it were, human conscience laid out before us. What we see outside us may be considered as the picture of our inner life. The forces within ourselves may appear to have no relation to outer nature. But the truth is, bone can only be bone because it hates calcium carbonate and calcium phosphate in their mineral state, because it withdraws from them, contracting into itself, whereby it becomes something different from what these substances are in external nature. And one must be able to accept that for man to have a physical form, hatred and coldness must be present in his physical nature.

Through this, you see, our words gain inner significance. It is good for our bones to have a certain hardness; they have it as a physical image of spiritual coldness. But it is not good for our social life if our souls have this hardness. The physical nature of man must be different from his soul nature. Man is able to be man precisely because his physical being differs from his soul and spirit. Man's physical nature also differs from physical nature around him. On this rests the necessity for transformation about which I have spoken to you.

All this forms an important supplement to what I once said in the course on Cosmology, Philosophy and Religion about man's connection with the hierarchies.* It could only be added, however, on such initial considerations as those in our present lectures. For spiritual vision gives insight alike into what the separate members of the mineral, animal and plant kingdoms really are here on earth, and into the work of the hierarchies—work that continues from age to age, as do also the processes that occur in the physical world and the works of man.

When man's life between death and a new birth—his life in the spiritual world—is beheld in this way, one can describe his experiences in that world in just as much detail as his biography here on earth. So we may live in the hope that, when we pass through the gate of death, all that we take into the world of the spirit as lack of understanding and human hatred may be given back to us again, and ennobled through human forms being created from it.

In the course of long centuries something very strange has come to pass, however, for the present stage of human evolution. It no longer proved possible to use up all the forces of human lack of understanding and human hatred and make them into new human forms in the world of the spirit. Something was left over. In the course of the last centuries this residue has streamed down on to the earth, so that in the spiritual atmosphere of the earth, in what I may call the earth's astral light, there is to be found an infiltration of the impulses of human hatred and human contempt, impulses that exist exterior to man. These have not been incorporated into human forms; they stream around the earth in the astral light. They influence man—not individual human beings but the relationships which people form with one another on the earth. They influence civilization. And within civilization they

---

* Rudolf Steiner. *Philosophy, Cosmology and Religion.* Ten lectures given at the Goetheanum in September, 1922. Anthroposophic Press, New York 1984.

have brought about what compelled me to say, in the spring of 1914 in Vienna,* that our present-day civilization is invaded by a spiritual cancer, by spiritual ulcers.

At the time—I spoke of this in the lecture course dealing with the phenomena occurring between death and a new birth—people did not like hearing it. Since then, however, some of the truth of what was said has been recognized. At the time people had no awareness of what streams through civilization. They did not perceive that actual cancerous formations were present in civilization, for it was only from 1914 onwards that these erupted. Today they are revealed as utterly diseased tissues of civilization. It is possible to see everything that lives in a civilization as an integral spiritual entity. And we find that in this modern civilization of ours, which has been infiltrated by the currents of human hatred and human coldness not used up in human forms, those currents have become the parasitic element of modern civilization.

Civilization has profoundly parasitic tendencies today; it is like a part of an organism that is invaded by parasites, by bacilli. What people have amassed in the way of thoughts exists, but it has no living connection with man. Only consider how this shows itself in the most ordinary phenomena of daily life. People have to learn because things are there to be learned; they do not bring enthusiasm to their learning but simply have to get down to it and learn in order to pass an examination, so as to qualify for some particular post, or the like—well, for them there is no vital connection between what they have to take in and what lives in their soul as an inborn desire for the things of the mind and spirit. It is exactly as though a person who is not predisposed to hunger were to be continually stuffing himself with food! The food does not go

---

* Rudolf Steiner. *The Inner Nature of Man and Our Life Between Death and Rebirth.* Eight lectures given in Vienna in April 1914. Rudolf Steiner Press, London 1994.

through the transformations about which I have spoken, it turns into ballast in the organism, finally becoming something which literally invites parasites.

Much in our modern civilization has no connection with man. Like the mistletoe—spiritually speaking—it lives on what man brings forth from the original impulses of his mind and heart. Much of this manifests in our civilization as parasitic existence. To anyone who has the power of seeing our civilization with spiritual vision, in the astral light, as it were, the year 1914 already presented an advanced stage of cancer, a tumour; for him the whole of civilization was already invaded by parasites. But then something further is added to this parasitic condition.

I have described to you in what may be called a spiritual physiology how the nature of the gnomes and undines, who work from below upwards, gives rise to the possibility of parasitic impulses in man. Then, however, as I explained, the opposite picture presents itself in contrast—for poison is carried downwards by the sylphs and the elemental beings of warmth. And so in a civilization like ours, which bears a parasitic character, what comes down from above—spiritual truth, though not poison in itself, is transformed into poison in man, so that our civilization rejects it in fear and invents all kinds of reasons for this rejection. The two things belong together: a parasitic culture below, which does not proceed from elemental laws and therefore contains parasites within itself; and spirituality that comes down from above and as it enters into civilization is taken up by man in such a way that it becomes poison. When you bear this in mind you have the key to the most important symptoms of modern civilization. And when one has insight into these things, the necessary educational aspect will, of its own accord, reveal itself as the right medicine for our civilization. Just as a rational therapy evolves from a true diagnosis, a true pathology of the individual, so a diagnosis of the sickness of a civilization reveals the remedy; the one calls forth the other.

It is very evident that mankind today again needs a kind of civilization that comes really close to the human heart and the human soul, and springs directly from the human heart and the human soul. If a child, on entering primary school, is introduced to a highly sophisticated system of letter forms which he has to learn as a ... b ... c, etc., he does not relate to this in heart and soul. He has no relation to them at all. What the child develops in his head, in his heart and soul, by having to learn a ... b ... c, is—spiritually speaking—a parasite in human nature.

During his years of education a great deal is brought to the child of this parasitic nature. We must, therefore, develop an art of education that works creatively from his soul. We must let the child give form to colours; and the colour forms that have arisen out of joy, out of disappointment, out of every possible feeling, these he can put on paper: pleasure and pain. When a child puts on paper what arises out of his soul, this develops his humanity. This produces nothing parasitic. This is something which grows out of man like his fingers or his nose!—whereas, when the letters of the alphabet, which are the product of advanced civilization, are imposed on the human being, this does engender a parasitic element.

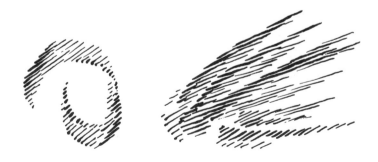

The moment the art of education lies close to the human heart, to the human soul, the spiritual can be brought to man without becoming poison. First you have the diagnosis, which finds that our age is infested with carcinomas, and then you have the therapy—yes, it is Waldorf School education.

Waldorf School education is founded upon nothing other than this, my dear friends. Here the thinking about the cultural sphere is the same as that applied in the field of medicine. This is the specific application of what I spoke about a few days ago, namely, that the being of man progresses to the development of the spiritual from below upwards, from nutrition through healing, and that one must regard education as medicine transposed into the realm of mind and spirit. This strikes us with particular clarity when we wish to find a therapy for civilization, for we can only conceive this therapy as being Waldorf School education.

You will readily be able to imagine the feelings of one who not only has insight into this situation, but who is also trying to develop Waldorf School education in a practical way, when he sees the general effect of this carcinoma of civilization giving rise to conditions in Central Europe that may seriously endanger this Waldorf School education, or even make it altogether impossible. We should not reject such thoughts as these, but rather make them the impulse within ourselves to work together wherever we still can in the therapy of our civilization.

During my Helsingfors (Helsinki) lecture course in 1913,* I expressed from a certain perspective of spiritual knowledge a view about the inferior nature of Woodrow Wilson, who then became a veritable object of veneration for much of civilized mankind and in respect of whom people are only now—

---

* Rudolf Steiner. *The Occult Significance of the Bhagavad Gita.* Nine lectures given in Helsingfors in May and June 1913. Anthroposophic Press, New York 1968.

because to do otherwise is impossible—gaining some measure of perception. As things went then, so have things also gone in regard to the carcinoma of civilization about which I spoke in Vienna. Well, that is how these things went; today the same holds true for the things that apply in our time. People are asleep. It is time, however, that we woke up. And anthroposophy bears within it all the impulses for a real awakening of civilization and culture, for man's true cultural awakening!

This is what I wished to say to you in the last of these lectures.

Publisher's Note Regarding Rudolf Steiner's Lectures

The lectures and addresses contained in this volume have been translated from the German, which is based on steno-graphic and other recorded texts that were in most cases never seen or revised by the lecturer. Hence, due to human errors in hearing and transcription, they may contain mistakes and faulty passages. Every effort has been made to ensure that this is not the case. Some of the lectures were given to audiences more familiar with anthroposophy; these are the so-called 'private' or 'members' lectures. Other lectures, like the written works, were intended for the general public. The difference between these, as Rudolf Steiner indicates in his *Autobiography*, is twofold. On the one hand, the lectures given to members of the Anthroposophical Society take for granted a background in and commitment to anthroposophy; in the public lectures this was not the case. At the same time, the members' lectures address the concerns and dilemmas of the members, while the public work speaks directly out of Steiner's own understanding of universal needs. Never-theless, as Rudolf Steiner stresses: 'Nothing was ever said that was not solely the result of my direct experience of the growing content of anthroposophy. There was never any question of concessions to the prejudices and preferences of the members. Whoever reads these privately printed lectures can take them to represent anthroposophy in the fullest sense. Thus it was possible without hesitation—when the complaints in this direction became too persistent—to depart from the custom of circulating this material "for members only". But it must be borne in mind that faulty passages do occur in these reports not revised by myself.' Earlier in the same chapter, he states: 'Had I been able to correct them [the private lectures], the restriction *for members only* would have been unnecessary from the beginning.'